A Chris

A Christian Approach to the Environment

THE·JOHN·RAY·INITIATIVE
connecting environment, science and Christianity

Published 2005 by *The John Ray Initiative* (www.jri.org.uk)

First published in the journal *Transformation* (An International Evangelical Dialogue on Mission and Ethics): R C J & M A Carling (guest editors) 'A Christian Approach to the Environment' *Transformation* Vol 16 No 3, July/September 1999

ISBN: 0-9550878-0-5

© The John Ray Initiative 2005

All rights reserved. No part of this publication may be reproduced in any form, stored in or re-introduced into a retrieval system, or transmitted, in any form or by any means, electronic, mechanical, photocopying, recording or otherwise without the prior written permission of the publisher or a licence permitting restricted copying. In the UK such licences are issued by the Copyright Licensing Agency, 90 Tottenham Court Road, London W1P 9HE

A full CIP record for this book is available from the British Library

Compiled and typeset by Dr R C J Carling
Printed by Guilder Graphics Ltd

Contents

Foreword		
	– Lord Carey	vi
Introduction		vii
1.	A Christian approach to the environment – Sam Berry	1
2.	Why aren't more church people interested in the environment? – Hugh Montefiore	5
3.	Recovering the 'Creation': A response to Hugh Montefiore – Alister McGrath	19
4.	Theology and ethics of the land – Chris Wright	29
5.	The Old Testament and the environment: A response to Chris Wright – Gordon Wenham	49
6.	The New Testament teaching on the environment – Ernest Lucas	73
7.	The New Testament teaching on the environment: A response to Ernest Lucas – Richard Bauckham	97
8.	Christians, environment and society – Michael Northcott	105
9.	Christians, environment and society: A response to Michael Northcott – Chris Sugden	133
Epilogue		
	– John Houghton	143

Foreword

It is at last beginning to dawn on many people that an environmental disaster confronts our tiny and overcrowded planet. Regretfully, the Christian voice has been, at times, subdued in giving expression to the positive and strong features of a Christian theology of nature. However, it is to the credit of Sir John Houghton and Dr Bob Carling and their colleagues that they have not been reticent or silent. An example lies in this short collection of essays where a fascinating and deep conversation opens up among the contributors, illustrating that the Christian gospel is still able to speak compellingly to modern issues and questions.

The Rt Hon. the Lord Carey of Clifton

Introduction

This book was originally published as a special issue of the journal *Transformation* and the chapters were based on papers presented at a consultation meeting organised by The John Ray Initiative held at the Brunei Centre, University of London, Saturday, 20 February 1999.

The special issue of the journal became adopted on courses – 'Christian Rural and Environmental Studies', Gloucester University, UK and 'Christian Faith and the Environment', Open Theological College – and so it was decided that it should be made available in book form, both for these courses and for a wider audience.

Sadly, as the book went to press Hugh Montefiore, one of the contributors to the book, died. He was a tireless Christian environmentalist and will be sorely missed.

We are delighted to have an endorsement for the book by Lord Carey, who as well as being a previous Archbishop of Canterbury is also the Chancellor of Gloucester University, where The John Ray Initiative is based.

The John Ray Initiative

1 – A Christian approach to the environment

Sam Berry

> Professor R.J. (Sam) Berry FRSE is Professor of Genetics at University College London
>
> Creation care has for a long time been a low priority for the church. The consultation reported on in this issue explored the reasons for this and reviewed a theological understanding of creation.
>
> **Keywords:** environment, stewardship, The John Ray Initiative

The Bible teaching on the environment is very straightforward:

1. We live in a world that belongs to God; He made, redeemed and sustains it.
2. God has entrusted the care of this creation to us; we are trustees, stewards, managers – no word conveys the full meaning of the ordinance laid on those upon whom God conferred His own image.
3. We will be held accountable for the way(s) in which we have exercised our responsibility.

None of these principles is obscure either in their original formulation in the Scriptures, nor in their restatements at various times in Christian history from at least the time of Irenaeus in the second century AD, through Benedict and his rule, to John Ray in the seventeenth century and many people alive today. Yet time and time again creation care has been such a low priority in the Church's agenda that it had been effectively non-existent. Plato's influence in the early Christian centuries directed gaze away from the dynamic realities of the living world; the Reformers concentration on the world as little more than the stage for God's saving work; the rationalism of the Enlightenment leading to the even greater sterility of the deists; the confusion about God's work in the world following the Darwinian revolution; distrust in the revealed Word producing the flailings of the mystics, New Age and others – all have marginalised and disembowelled the simple elements of biblical creation care.

Lynn White expressed the impotence and consequent damage wrought on the environment by Christians when he wrote, 'We shall continue to have a worsening ecological crisis until we reject the Christian axiom that nature has no reason for existence but to serve man ... Christianity ... insisted that it is God's will that man exploit nature for his proper ends ... Christianity bears a huge burden of guilt.'[1] White's thesis has been criticised by both historians and theologians, but it has had a wide influence and has been much repeated.[2]

But while Christians stood still – or at best cheered from the side-lines – the secular world has been stirred and then alarmed by ever increasing signs of environmental damage. The UK White Paper on the environment (*This Common Inheritance*, 1990) declared unequivocally, 'Whatever the discoveries of science, whatever the rate at which we multiplied as a species, whatever the changes we made to our seas and landscape, we have believed that the world would stay much the same in all its fundamentals.'[3] *This Common Inheritance* formed the official UK submission to the United Nations Conference on Environment and Development (UNCED) in 1992, the so-called 'Earth Summit'. At UNCED, the nations of the world committed themselves to common action on global environmental problems, albeit with sundry reservations, hesitations and qualifications.[4]

Meanwhile the World Council of Churches had added environment concerns to its longstanding commitment to peace with justice, and established a programme on 'Justice, Peace and the Integrity of Creation' (JPIC). After a series of regional consultations, a concluding conference was held at Seoul in 1990. It was not a happy occasion, with sectional and marginal interests dominating the reports.[5] In response, The World Evangelical Fellowship Unit on Ethics and Society convened a consultation in September 1992 at the Au Sable Institute in Michigan, USA to explore a more biblical agenda. Reports of the Au Sable meeting appeared in *Transformation* in October 1992 and April 1993, and as a special issue of the *Evangelical Review of Theology* in April 1993. These stimulated thoughts and prayers in different parts of the world, and, although not a direct consequence of JPIC and Au Sable, The John Ray Initiative was set up in 1998.[6]

The stated vision of The John Ray Initiative is 'to bring together scientific and Christian understandings of the environment in a way that can be widely communicated and lead to effective action; it aims to promote a deeper understanding of the environment and how humankind should relate to it, based on observation, study and an ethical approach to decision making and stewardship.' In crude terms this means educating Christians about creation care as a mainstream obligation on all believers, not merely a hobby for a small minority or a pantheistic option for those inclined to doctrinal wooliness. It implies also that Christians should be working alongside others in environmental stewardship as partners but additionally as evangelists, proclaiming that *all things* were reconciled to God by Christ's shedding of his blood on the cross (Colossians 1:20).[7]

The John Ray Initiative is training Christians in environmental knowledge and theology so that they can 'teach others also'. It is also exploring ways with both theologians and technologists about developing deeper understanding of environmental theology and ethics as a contribution to scholarship, but, more importantly, to action. The papers in this issue of *Transformation* were given at an invited consultation in London on 20 February 1999. The consultation had a two-fold purpose: to review and explore the theological understanding of creation and our response to this understanding both as individuals and as communities (church and secular); and to discuss why Christians have generally failed to take seriously the theological imperative to care for the earth. The eight papers herein were pre-circulated to all those who attended the London consultation; we hope this wider availability will further the discussion and commitment which gripped those present in London.

Notes

1. White, L. 'The historical roots of our ecologic crisis'. *Science*, 1967, 155: 1204–1207.
2. For example, Francis Schaeffer reprinted White's essay in its entirety in his *Pollution and the Death of Man*, London: Hodder & Stoughton, 1970, commenting favourably on it.
3. *This Common Inheritance: Britain's Environmental Strategy*. Cm 1200. London: HMSO, 1990.
4. Grubb, M., Koch, M., Munson, A., Sullivan, F. and Thomson, K. *The Earth Summit Agreements*. London: Earthscan, 1993.
5. See reports in *Transformation*, July 1990.
6. Further information about The John Ray Initiative can be obtained from: Dr John Sale, JRI Executive Secretary, Fach Gynan, Moelfre, Oswestry SY10 7QP, United Kingdom. Tel/Fax: +44(01691)791404. Email: info@jri.org.uk. http://www.jri.org.uk.
7. Berry, R.J. 'Creation and the environment.' *Science and Christian Belief*, 1995, 7: 21–43; Berry R.J. 'A worldwide ethic for sustainable living.' *Ethics, Place and Environment*, 1999, 2: 97–107.

2 – Why aren't more church people interested in the environment?

Hugh Montefiore

> The Rt Revd Hugh Montefiore DD was formerly Bishop of Birmingham
>
> There are several historical reasons for the lack of interest in environmental issues – several specifically unique for Christians.
>
> **Keywords:** environment, Anglican Church, Board for Social Responsibility.

I shall begin by trying to answer this question in a rather personal way. My own concern about the environment began when I was a curate in Newcastle-upon-Tyne way back in 1951. I read a book by a Geordie, Michael Roberts, who had followed up a popular book on the *Decline of the West* with a less popular one called *The Estate of Man*. Roberts was a man of many parts who was Principal of the Church Training College of St John and St Mark in Chelsea. The blurb of the book asserted that even in the 1950s the picture was a sombre one, but claimed that the arguments would be difficult to contest concerning deforestation, exhaustion of the soil and steady increase of desert and the plundering of mineral wealth, making us apprehensive of the future of the human race. Other writers had warned of particular problems, but Roberts, so far as I know, was the first person in this country to bring together their conclusions, and to warn of future deterioration in a highly industrialised and urban society. It has to be said that most of his statistics have proved to be wrong, but most of his conclusions have been shown to be right. And, let it be realised, Michael Roberts was a Christian.

I was hooked nearly half a century ago, and have been ever since. But this is an issue which, far from catching the popular imagination, worried practically no one. A lot has changed in forty eight years!

Environmental interest in the Anglican church

It took a decade before the Church of England began to be interested. Fortunately Mr Edwin Barker, then Secretary of the Board for Social Responsibility under the old Church Assembly, was deeply concerned. He got his Chairman, Bishop Williams, to publish a collection of essays on *The Responsible Church* in 1961, and invited me to write a chapter on the environment. I was by this time a don in Cambridge, and had been busy collecting material for a book I published in 1969 which I called *The Question Mark*[1] (the question being the survival of the human race). It is an interesting commentary on the state of awareness in the nation as a whole that the Editor of the *New Scientist* described it as 'being quite unique in being so well informed'. Yet I had done no original research!

Meanwhile Edwin Barker had been getting together a group which published in 1970 a report called *Man in His Living Environment: An Ethical Assessment*.[2] The Board was encouraged to set up this group by the Standing Committee of the 'Countryside in 1970' Conferences which the Duke of Edinburgh chaired and which helped to make some people aware that there was a problem. I remember the debate in the Church Assembly when Lancelot Fleming, the Bishop of Norwich, introduced the church's report. There was some interest, but the Church Assembly was hardly ever able to show any actual excitement. This was the period when the Government set up its Standing Royal Commission on the Pollution of the Environment. I remember asking for an interview with Antony Crosland, at that time Secretary of State for the Environment. 'Why is there no churchman on it?' I asked him. 'I never thought of it' he replied, 'Whom would you suggest?' I put forward the name of Bishop Lancelot Fleming and was rather surprised to find that he was duly appointed.

At this time I was a member of the Archbishops' Commission on Christian Doctrine, and I persuaded Archbishop Ramsey to ask the Commission to set a small group of its members to consider the theology of the environment. In 1975 there was published a report called *Man and Nature*,[3] which was, I think I am right in saying, the first official publication on environmental theology. Also in 1975 Bishop John Taylor of Winchester produced a very popular little book called *Enough is Enough*[4] but it was really about over consumption and did not tackle the serious environmental issues. I mention these historical details because it is I think important to realise that when environmental concerns surfaced earlier this century the Church as an institution was indeed involved, but it aroused little interest among its members.

Popular interest in environmental matters really began with the United Nations Conference held in Stockholm in 1972 and with Barbara Ward's best-selling paperback *Only One Earth*[5] which was written in preparation for it. Friends of the Earth began to achieve considerable publicity by their collection and dumping of empty glass bottles at the manufacturers' gates. The media began to take up environmental issues and by the 1980s the non-governmental organisations on the environment went from strength to strength. Not so the Churches. The early enthusiasms, such as they were, faded. Why was this? The Church became enmeshed in internal arguments, such as whether or not it was right to ordain women to the priesthood, or what measures, if any, we could agree for church reunion. There was little interest in ecological issues among the hierarchy. Edwin Barker had retired from the Board for Social Responsibility, and his successor was not interested. When I became a member of that Board, I suggested that it concerned itself with environmental issues, and I was told that it had enough to do without that. There were also other factors enumerated below. These attempts to arouse interest in ecology failed miserably: I was dubbed contemptuously in turn an 'eco-freak', an 'eco-priest' and finally an 'eco-bishop'.

Later, when I became Chairman of the Board for Social Responsibility, I did manage to set up an Environmental Panel to advise the Board, because its members (apart from

Professor R. J. Berry) had no expertise in these areas. A Synod report was produced, but the debate on it in the General Synod was lacklustre. In the 1970s I had undertaken, on behalf of the Ecological Foundation, an enquiry into transport, which even then was causing problems. Although our report was used at university level, it made little impact on the public and none on the government. The public however *was* rattled by the dangers of nuclear energy, partly because of the Cold War, with the danger that nuclear weapons might be used if the war got hot, and partly because the pollution properties of nuclear energy were invisible and therefore terrifying. It is no coincidence that one of the first Reports of the Standing Royal Commission was on this very subject. The British Council of Churches asked me to conduct a Hearing into the Fast Breeder Reactor with which we were at that time threatened. The Hearing took place off Fleet Street, but did not catch the imagination of the media, nor did the transcript which was later published. The World Council of Churches held a Hearing on Nuclear Energy in Situgna in Sweden, chaired by the Archbishop of York; but Sweden is too distant to have much impact in England. The World Council also held an enormous conference on Faith, Science and the Future at Massachusetts Institute of Technology in 1979 – but who cares what happens at conferences? When I came back, full of enthusiasm to broadcast its findings, I had to cancel meetings I had arranged because no-one was interested.

Reasons for lack of interest

During the last twenty years many books on environmental matters have been written, and there has been much talk. It is only in the last few years that anything important has happened politically, and practically nothing has been done by the Church, although I am happy to say that all parishes in the two dioceses of Southwark and in March this year were invited to carry out an environmental audit. One has to ask why the churches have lagged behind. In a famous article way back in 1967,[6] Lynn White had suggested that the exploitative attitude which has engendered the environmental crisis in Western industrialised nations is itself the direct result of the Judaeo–Christian tradition, with its basic Christian axiom that nature has no reason for its existence save to serve man. Although it was comparatively easy to show that White's generalisations were wild – St Francis and St Benedict for example were ecologists before their time – the lack of interest among churchmen does call for some explanation. I think there are several factors involved. First I will look at explanations which are common to Christians and others, and then later at explanations which concern Christians only.

1. People are not convinced that there are limits to growth, because it is easy to assume technological fixes by which shortages can be overcome. Something will turn up. Take for example the threatened rundown of some types of fossil fuels in the next century. Let me record what I have read in a single week. Gas globules have been discovered on the ocean bed: future technology will enable us to use this as out source of energy. Alternatively, some method will be discovered of extracting hydrogen from water which produces more energy than that used up by producing it; and technology will be found for its safe storage so that we shall be able to use a non-global warming hydrogen economy. The supreme example of the technological fix is Amory Lovins' claim that one could realistically envisage that, in the next fifty years, if world population doubled and per capita GDP increased threefold or fourfold, we could find at the same time the technology to reduce carbon intensity twofold and we could reduce total energy use eighteenfold. When people read that kind of thing – I found it in a current copy of Resurgence – ordinary people think: why worry? That applies to Christians as much as to anybody else.

2. Science and technology are very complex matter to the non-scientist; and even scientists are so specialised nowadays that most do not know about geophysiology. How can the ordinary person be expected to know whether or not the earth has the capacity to withstand our thoughtless use of its resources and our pollution of its air and earth and rivers and oceans? Of course the ordinary person can listen to the experts; but, alas, the experts often disagree. Because the media like controversy, and insist on 'balance', they tend to give equal publicity to those experts who believe that we are not endangering the earth's life-carrying capacity and those who believe that we are endangering it, even if the arguments of the former are weak compared to those of the latter. When experts disagree, how can the ordinary person make up his or her mind on the matter? Of course there is the precautionary principle, that it is wise to take precautions in case those who believe that we are endangering life on earth happen to be right. But the type of precautions required would be expensive and would be bound to result in our changing our lifestyle, so the principle does not get much of a look-in, especially when the government, which claims to be green, tells people through their panels of experts that all is well; carrots are safe to eat, and genetically modified food will do no one any harm, etc. Christians on the whole are particularly susceptible to feeling that they are not in a position to take up an unpopular position on environmental issues. On the whole they are a bit frightened of science, and – with a few outstanding exceptions – they do not know much about environmental matters. To take a stand might expose them as ignorant and panicky. It would be more prudent, they think, to leave this kind of thing to others.

3. I mentioned that the type of precautions required to ensure that we do not make life difficult for posterity, and to prevent us endangering the future of life on earth would result in a change in our lifestyle. We live in a very materialist society, and most people are not prepared to give up the search for an ever increasing standard of living, especially in a country which has the largest proportion of people living below the poverty line in Western Europe. Christian people are bound to be affected by the prevailing ethos. Some Christians would certainly be willing to have a lower standard of living if this were the penalty imposed on them for being Christian. But most Christians in the Western World today enjoy as much as anyone else their washing machines and cars and other labour saving comforts which increase their standard of living, and they are unwilling to campaign against the prevailing ethos, for fear of being thought hypocrites. One only has to look around at churches and church people in the Western World to see that they have been greatly affected by materialism.

4. Population growth is intimately involved with the degradation of our environment, and the fact that mankind is commanded in Genesis to be fruitful and multiply has, I think, warned off a lot of Christians from environmental issues. I think that this especially applies to the Roman Catholic Church, which has studiously downplayed environmental issues in the past with only a few passing references in recent papal encyclicals or apostolic letters. Only this February the Pontifical Council for the Family stated that the so-called population explosion is the 'inane' invention of the media, that the UN is forcing developing countries to enforce 'Malthusian' policies, and that nongovernmental organisations such as the International Planned Parenthood Federation are supporting policies of enforced sterilisation of women, and condoning coercive birth control measures (which incidentally it is not). The Roman Catholic Church is the largest church in the world, and so its utterances on this subject are important, although if is doubtful how many of its adherents take note in private of its statements on birth control; but they do not like to oppose them publicly. In fact our planet will have 6 billion people next year, compared with 2 billion in the 1930s, and although the fertility rate is now slowing down, nonetheless 700 million young people in the developing countries will join the workforce during the next decade, a number more than the entire workforce of the developed countries in 1990. However, population is declining in the Western World, and in Britain it is below replacement level, so this particular issue seems irrelevant to people in Britain, who can only stand by – as they think, helplessly – as numbers in the developing world increase.

5. Britain is a very insular country, as has often been remarked. It is what happens in Britain rather than in the rest of the world which really matters, not only in population issues but in other spheres as well. In the 1998 report of the Worldwatch Institute in Washington, its President wrote:

> From 1950 to 1997 the use of lumber tripled, that of paper increased sixfold, the fish catch increased nearly fivefold, grain consumption nearly tripled, fossil fuel burning nearly quadrupled, and air and water pollutants multiplied several-fold ... Forests are shrinking, water tables are falling, soils are eroding, wetlands are disappearing, fisheries are collapsing, rangelands are deteriorating, rivers are running dry, temperatures are rising, coral reefs are dying and plant and animal species are disappearing.

But in Britain, everything seems alright. The soil does not seem to be deteriorating, the rivers are not running dry, there is still plenty of mackerel in the shops, the Fens are still full of water, the beaches are getting cleaner. We only wish that the temperature would rise a little more, and animal and plant species seem to be doing very nicely thank you. People do not realise that ecology knows no frontiers, and that we are all interdependent. They do not ask themselves whether it is the excessive demand on resources overseas by the Western nations which is causing most of the ecological damage. People in Britain feel that things cannot be as bad as they are made out to be. They do not connect cutting down tropical forests with buying furniture for their newly mortgaged houses. Hamburgers are too popular for many people to protest about rain forests being cut down to produce short-term pasture for the production of the meat that goes into them.

The five reasons I have so far adduced are common to Christians and most of the rest of the population. In the UK Christians usually do not stand out from others in most of their habits, so these reasons are important for them too. I turn now to reasons why Christians in particular tend to be disinterested in environmental issues.

6. There is no direct mention of the environment in the Scriptures, because in the days when they were written there were different environmental problems. If people then did not assert their dominion over animals, the animals asserted their dominion over people! Our problems have arisen only recently through exponential growth in human population and through the increased use of material resources made possible by the advances of science and technology. The Old Testament, because it legislates for a theocracy, contains rules for the treatment of the land at the jubilee (Leviticus 25), but the point here is not so much the conservation of the earth as that the land belongs to God, and not to us human beings. There are also regulations for the treatment of domesticated animals, and about how to treat birds nests and so on; but this hardly adds up to an environmental ethic. In the second creation story in Genesis, Adam was placed in charge of the garden of Eden, but the point here is not that he must tend it as an ecosystem as that he must obey the rules of its Master, and not eat apples. Certainly in the prophetic books there is a link between disobedience to God and ecological disaster, but once again this does not in itself imply the need for conservation.

When we turn to the New Testament, there is little in Jesus's reported words to suppose that the environment was a matter of great concern. Certainly, he remarked on the beauty of wild flowers, and on the value of even a sparrow in the sight of God; but these in themselves do not add up to environmental concern. Jesus did not preach about rocks or the air or the soil, but about the Kingdom of God, and few people see the connection between the two. The early Christians were, if I may use the term, Christ-intoxicated, and so their message was focused on the ministry, death and resurrection of Christ, not on the environment.

7. The fact that humanity was given dominion over the whole of the natural world has also inhibited interest in environmental matters. Here we must admit some truth in the accusation of Lynn White. Christians on the whole have not connected this grant of dominion with the fact that humanity is also made in the image of God, and therefore must always behave responsibly towards the natural world. It took a long time for a consensus in this country to arrive that we should not be cruel to animals, and the same could not yet be said of many other countries. The world is here for the use of humanity, it was assumed, and we should make as much use of it as we can. Furthermore, it used to be thought that the whole world was under the evil one. Humanity had fallen, and not only humanity but all things living. Creation as a whole needed to be redeemed. If the natural world is so evil, it follows that humanity can do what it likes with it. It can exploit it, rape it, damage it, because it is evil. I do not believe that this attitude is common today, although we still tend to think of the world as God's gift for our exploitation. When such an attitude first hardened, there was no thought that species could be endangered or ecosystems could be broken down, and that resources were limited. Today, even if we no longer think of the world as fallen, and despite the fact that nowadays we have a better understanding of humanity's dominion, our practice has not changed much. We are a very traditional people, and we tend to keep on in our old ways.

8. Many Christians think that their energies should be taken up not with such matters as the environment, but with spreading the Good News of Jesus Christ. How to cope with environmental issues is not, they think, remotely connected with spreading the Gospel. It seems to have nothing to do with Jesus Christ. He never spoke about it. Jesus did not die to make the environment safe: he died to save our souls. There is much crypto- Gnosticism in contemporary Christianity. It is about spiritual matters: the state of our souls, our receptivity and openness to God, our repentance for what we have done wrong. It is about the goodness and the graciousness of God. It is not about our putting right the environment in which we live. Christian ethics are about how we behave to one another, and whether we obey the commandments of God, and not about the way we treat the non-human creation. Stewardship is about the way we deal with our own possessions, and how much we give to the church, not about the way in which we treat our common inheritance of the earth on which we live. I have put this crudely, and I am sure that many people think in a more sophisticated manner about the environment. But at root this is, I believe, how many Christians feel. They focus not on creation but on salvation.

9. Those Christians who do believe that the Gospel compels them to take note of what is happening in the world tend to concentrate on social issues. So far as the Church of England is concerned (I know that the Church of Scotland has been more environmentally minded, but the Church of England is the only church I really know) there is not a lot of energy left over from running a vast church institution with less people involved in it, and from spreading the Christian faith and joining in the social life of the local Christian community. What energy there is left over tends to go on helping people rather than helping the planet. One World Week and Christian Aid and Tear Fund are the kind of charities which people willingly give themselves to help; and of course there are plenty of other charities, churchy or non-churchy, to which people give their energies. There is much in the New Testament about helping our neighbours, and while people are able to extend the meaning of neighbour to people overseas in desperate need, they do not extend the concept to the natural world as a whole. The environment has very low priority, except when the NIMBY factor is involved (the acronym standing of course for 'Not In My Back Yard'). Things must take second place to People. However, people do not realise that unless we give due attention to things, there may not be any people!

10. Those Christians who do feel that they ought to do something about the environment, other than NIMBY issues, are often put off by a feeling of helplessness. The issues are so big, and the influence of an individual is so small. Human nature being what it is, government regulation is needed to restrain over consumption and pollution. How can an individual influence government issues? In fact organisations like Friends of the Earth do this, but Christians often feel that they ought to join a specifically Christian organisation, rather than put their energy into a secular NGO. (As a former chairman of the Friends of the Earth Trust and Transport2000, it is not a conviction which I share.) Christians can make a difference when they reach across church frontiers and join together in a common cause, as they have done over Third World debt. They could do the same with environmental issues.

11. One of the reasons why some Christians do not like to join a secular organisation over environmental issues is that they fear that they are joining forces with adherents of the New Age movement. Christian tends to emphasise so much the majesty and transcendence of Almighty God that they forget that his Holy Spirit is the Lord and Giver of life, and that God is immanent in the world as well as transcendent over it. This makes them all the more likely to mistrust the New Age movement, and they have good reason to do so. Although very varied in its membership, New Age does tend to be pantheist in it presuppositions, and some of its members appear to worship the earth as a goddess. While all life is certainly interdependent, and all life is worthy of respect, New

Agers tend to put flora and fauna on the same level as human beings. Some Christians feel (wrongly) that to be concerned about the environment is likely to embroil them in New Age philosophy. They forget that it is sometimes necessary to associate with people with whom we disagree in order to achieve a common goal.

12. More important than campaigning on particular issues is to change the basic attitudes of people in this country on environmental matters, and to see these as an integral part of preparing for the coming of God's kingdom. The Church, however, is not in a position to do this, because the bulk of its adherents have not yet changed their own attitudes on these issues. How will they do so? Mostly through the preaching they hear and the books they read. So it is vital to have good popular books which encourage people to change their attitudes, and good popular preaching which inspires people to alter. This does not happen. As far as reading is concerned, the best and most profound theological books on the environment come from overseas, with thinkers such as Jürgen Moltmann in Germany, Leonardo Boff in Brazil and Sally MacFague in the USA. On the whole, few British people read books by foreign theologians, even when they are translated into English. As a result, we have few good books for popular consumption in this country which explain why caring for the environment is part of the Gospel, and which show that it is as important to be co-creators with God as it is to so-operate with God our Redeemer, and indeed that redeeming the earth is part of the work of redemption. We have lost our ancient Christian insight that all things are inter-related. As a result there are few compelling sermons preached by clergy and lay readers on the need to change our attitudes and our priorities about the environment. If only this could be achieved, the whole position would be transformed.

Notes

1. Montefiore, H. *The Question Mark*. London: Collins, 1969.

2. *Man in His Living Environment: An Ethical Assessment*, a Report for the Board for Social Responsibility, London: Church Information Office, 1970.
3. Montefiore, H. *Man and Nature*. London: Collins, 1975.
4. Taylor, J.V. *Enough is Enough*. London: SCM, 1975.
5. Ward, B. & Dubos, R. *Only One Earth*. London: Penguin, 1972.
6. White, L. 'The historical roots of our ecologic crisis.' *Science*, 1967, 155: 1204–1207.

3 – Recovering the 'Creation': A response to Hugh Montefiore
Alister E. McGrath

> The Revd Dr Alister E. McGrath is Principal of Wycliffe Hall, Oxford
>
> The doctrine of creation needs to be recovered. The 'image of God', and pictures of God being the master craftsman or builder, are used to analyse the biblical notion of creation, comparing it with the rise of modern technology – the desire to 'control'.
>
> **Keywords:** creation, environment, image of God

Bishop Montefiore's very helpful and perceptive paper shows both his longstanding concern for environmental issues, and also a considerable degree of thoughtful reflection on why Christians have generally failed to get involved in these matters.

The most helpful response is to take his discussion further. Bishop Montefiore has identified a number of factors that appear to hold us back from getting involved in this matter; I would like to identify a number of counterbalancing considerations which ought to encourage us to take these matters rather more seriously that we have in the past. Hopefully identification of both some factors which have held us back and others which ought to propel us forward will serve to help us become more involved in these issues.

I shall offer a consensual theological analysis, focusing on the doctrine of creation (see, for example, references 1–11). This particular doctrine is of compelling importance to our discussions of this theme, and it does us no harm to inject a little theology into our discussion! The general lines of approach which I shall adopt are the common heritage of Christianity, and do not reflect any particular emphasis within the Christian tradition. As I myself adopt an evangelical perspective, I shall, however, be particularly concerned to stress the biblical dimensions of this important matter.

The doctrine of creation builds on the great themes of Genesis 1–2, which stress that God created every aspect of the world, including ourselves. Yet other biblical themes are also important, including the idea that God imposes order upon chaos (see, for example, Isaiah 29:16; 44:8; Jeremiah 18:1–6).

The Genesis creation account reminds us that everything in this world is the work of God. Many in the Ancient Near East believed that the sun and moon were gods, and were fearful of them. They had to be worshipped in the right way; if they were not, they might withhold their light and plunge the world into darkness. Christians do not need to fear the sun or moon. They were created by God (Genesis 1:14–18), and are under his authority.

We also learn that men and women have been created in the image of God (Genesis 1:26–27). This distinguished human beings from all other created beings. Being created 'in the image of God' includes the ability to relate to God. In other words, God creates us with the intention of establishing a personal relationship between himself and us. To have the 'image of God' implies some kind of likeness between ourselves and God – but not an identity. We are not divine; rather, we are created for the purpose of relating to God. Sin frustrates that purpose, which is only realised through the redemption brought by Christ. Christ's saving death allows us to enter into this cherished and transforming relationship with God.

Two analogies are helpful as we attempt to make sense of this important doctrine. The first is to think of God as a builder or a master craftsman. We can think of God as both an architect and a builder – someone who both designed and constructed a beautiful building. The wisdom of God can thus be seen in the marvellous way in which the world is put together.

St Paul's Cathedral, London, is one of the greatest works of the architect Sir Christopher Wren. There is no memorial to

Wren in that cathedral – just an inscription over its north door: *Si monumentum requiris, circumspice* – 'If you are looking for a memorial, look around you'. The genius and wisdom of the architect can be seen in what he built. So we can see God's wisdom in the creation. 'The heavens declare the glory of God!' (Psalm 19:1).

The second helpful analogy is that of an artist – perhaps a famous painter or sculptor. Something of the artist's personality and genius can be seen in the work of art itself. In the same way, the wisdom and love of God can be seen in the beauty of creation. It is thus no wonder that so many natural scientists are active Christian believers. To study creation in such detail is to come into close contact with the works of God himself.

But what difference does this make to the way we think and act? There must be a connection between theology and lifestyle – between what we believe, and the way we behave. James asks us to be doers and not merely hearers of the word (James 1:22). So what difference does the doctrine of creation make to the attitude of Christian's to the environment?

The first point of relevance is that the doctrine of creation makes is that the world belongs to God. It is not ours. We did not make it. Adam was placed in the Garden of Eden to take care of it (Genesis 2:15). This is a vitally important insight. We are the *stewards* not the *owners* of God's creation. God has entrusted his good creation to us, and will hold us accountable for the use which we make of it.

This insight underlies a proper Christian concern for the environment. We are called to be earth-keepers, people who tend what God has made and entrusted to us. We simply do not have the right to exploit the world for our own profit. It is God's, not ours. As Adam was called to tend Eden, so we are called to share in this creation mandate. This insight must change the way we behave towards creation, and encourage us to respect and care for it as God's treasured possession.

The biblical notion of creation is enormously rich and complex, and offers a number of insights of determinative importance in relation to the issue of the care of creation. The following points emerge from any responsible attempt to take the biblical insights concerning creation seriously:

1. The natural order, including humanity, is the result of God's act of creation, and is affirmed to be God's possession.

2. Humanity is distinguished from the remainder of creation in terms of being created in the 'image of God'.

3. Humanity is charged with the tending of creation (as Adam was entrusted with the care of Eden), in the full knowledge that this creation is the cherished possession of God.

4. There is thus no theological ground for asserting that humanity has the 'right' to do what it pleases with the natural order. The creation is God's, and has been entrusted to humanity, who are to act as its steward, not its exploiter.

It is important to notice how the creation narratives can function as the basis of a rigorously- grounded approach to ecology (see, for example, reference 9). This has been set out in a particularly attractive manner in a recent study by Calvin B. DeWitt, where he argued that four fundamental ecological principles can readily be discerned within the biblical narratives.[12]

1. The 'earthkeeping principle': just as the creator keeps and sustains humanity, so humanity must keep and sustain the creator's creation.

2. The 'sabbath principle': the creation must be allowed to recover from human use of its resources.

3. The 'fruitfulness principle': the fecundity of the creation is to be enjoyed, not destroyed.

4. The 'fulfilment and limits principle': there are limits set to humanity's role within creation, with boundaries set in place which must be respected.

In making such basic points, it must be noted that they have generally failed to be noted within the more sceptical sections of the scientific community, who persist in portraying Christianity as lending some kind of ideological sanction to the unprincipled and unlimited exploitation of the environment. In 1967, Lynn White published an influential article in which he asserted that Christianity was to blame for the emerging ecological crisis on account of its using the concept of the 'image of God', found in the Genesis creation account (Genesis 1:26–27), as a pretext for justifying human exploitation of the world's resources.[13] Genesis, he argued, legitimated the notion of human domination over the creation, hence leading to its exploitation. Despite (or perhaps on account of?) its historical and theological superficiality, the paper had a profound impact on the shaping of popular scientific attitudes towards Christianity in particular, and religion in general.

With the passage of time, a more sanguine estimation of White's argument has gained the ascendancy (summarised by Whitney[14]). The argument is now recognised to be seriously flawed. A closer reading of the Genesis text indicated that such themes as 'humanity as the steward of creation' and 'humanity as the partner of God' are indicated by the text, rather than that of 'humanity as the lord of creation'.[15,16] Furthermore, a careful study of the reception of this text within the Judeo-Christian tradition makes it clear that White's interpretation simply cannot be sustained.[17] Far from being the enemy of ecology, the doctrine of creation affirms the importance of human responsibility towards the environment. In a widely-read study, the noted Canadian writer Douglas John Hall stressed that the biblical concept of 'domination' was to be understood specifically in terms of 'stewardship'.[18] To put it simply: creation is not the possession of humanity; it is something which is to be seen as entrusted to humanity, which is responsible for its safekeeping and tending.[19,20]

A further contribution has been made by the noted German theologian Jürgen Moltmann (born 1926), noted for his concern to ensure the theologically rigorous application of Christian theology to social, political and environmental issues.[1,21] For example, in his 1985 work *God in Creation*, Moltmann argues that the exploitation of the world reflects the rise of technology, and seems to have little to do with specifically Christian teachings. Furthermore, he stresses the manner in which God can be said to indwell the creation through the Holy Spirit, so that the pillage of creation becomes an assault on God. On the basis of this analysis, Moltmann is able to offer a rigorously Trinitarian defence of a distinctively Christian ecological ethic. Such is the importance of this point that it merits further discussion.

A fundamental theme of modernism – a term which is usually taken to refer to the cultural mood which began to emerge towards the opening of the twentieth century – is its desire to control, perhaps seen at its clearest in the Nietzschean theme of 'will-to-power'. Humanity needs only the will to achieve autonomous self-definition; it need not accept what has been given to it, whether in nature or tradition. In principle, all can be mastered and controlled. This desire for liberation was often linked with the mythical figure of Prometheus, who came to be seen as a symbol of liberation in European literature.[22,23] The rise of technology was seen as paralleling Prometheus' theft of fire from the Gods. Limits were removed. Prometheus was now unbound, and humanity poised to enter a new era of autonomy and progress. The rise of technology was seen as a tool to allow humanity to control its environment, without the need to respect natural limitations.

If anything can be identified as the enemy of those who care for creation, it is the ruthless human tendency to exploit and the refusal to accept that limits have been set for human behaviour and activity. For Christians, a fundamental element of original sin (as described in Genesis 3) is a desire to be like God, and be set free from all the restraints of creatureliness. This resolute refusal to accept a properly constituted place within creation can easily be seen to be linked with the development of tools by which humanity is no longer obligated to operate under any form of moral or physical restraint. White's thesis is right in one sense: Genesis does indeed contain the key to human exploitation of the world. Yet that key lies in the fall of humanity and the refusal to acknowledge the limits of human competence and authority. If we are to regain the 'enormous bliss' of Eden (Milton), it must be through recognising our limitations as God's creatures, and more specifically our obligations to tend and care for God's good creation. That means at least a rediscovery of Genesis, and certainly a more attentive reading than that offered by Lynn White.

The doctrine of creation also allows us another significant insight. *The creation is God's, not God.* Some religions, including some forms of paganism which have enjoyed a fashionable revival in recent years, argue that nature is divine. Christians adopt a significantly different approach. Nature is created by God. It is not divine, but something of God's nature and character can be known through it.

We need to draw a line between the creator and the creation. Everything on our side of the line – including ourselves! – is God's creation, not something which is in itself divine. There is no place in Christianity for the worship of nature (a point made in detail by Paul in Romans 1–2). God alone is to be worshipped. Yet we must respect and care for nature as the work of the same God who loves and redeemed us. To love God is to love the works of God – including the creation.

My reason for developing this point has to do with a point which Bishop Montefiore did not have time to develop in his excellent paper – namely, that some Christians feel that a concern for creation has pagan overtones. Let me make it clear that a number of writers have indeed taken this line of argument, especially those wishing to revive the ancient idea of Gaia, the earth-goddess (see, for example, references 24 and 25). Yet a concern for the creation does not involve any notion of the divinization of nature. Nor does it require an appeal to such notions as 'pantheism' or the less problematic 'panentheism'. The issue is primarily that of ownership and responsibility. We do not, and should not, fall into any pagan ways of thinking in urging that we show greater concern for this world in which we live.

So what conclusions may we draw? We need to encourage people strongly to speak of 'creation' rather than 'nature'. The temptation to use language which conforms to the predominant idiom of the natural sciences must be conceded; nevertheless, it is important to allow Christian insights to penetrate this area of discourse. The language that we use is of importance, and we must aim to ensure that we way we speak about the world reflects and embodies our conviction that the world is God's, not ours; and that we are responsible to God for the use we make and the care we take of this world.

Bishop Montefiore pointed out that there are few compelling sermons preached on environmental themes, and calls for a change in this matter. Amen to that! I would only add that we need to bring out in our preaching and teaching that there is a seamless link between a right understanding of the doctrine of creation and a right attitude towards that creation. May we rediscover the doctrine of creation, and exult in both its insights and its implications!

Notes

1. Bouma-Prediger, S. 'Creation as the home of God: the doctrine of creation in the theology of Jürgen Moltmann.' *Calvin Theological Journal* 1997, 32: 72–90.
2. Brooke, G.J. 'Creation in the Biblical tradition.' *Zygon*, 1987, 22: 227–248.
3. Gilkey, L. *Maker of Heaven and Earth: the Christian Doctrine of Creation in the Light of Modern Knowledge.* Garden City: Doubleday, 1959.
4. Hartlieb, E. *Natur als Schöpfung: Studien zum Verhältnis von Naturbegriff und Schöpfungsverständnis bei Günter Altner, Sigurd M. Daecke, Hermann Dembowski und Christian Link.* Frankfurt am Main-Berlin: Peter Lang, 1996.
5. Leslie, J. 'Creation stories, religious and atheistic.' *International Journal for Philosophy of Religion*, 1993, 34: 65–77.

6. Lohfink, N. 'God the creator and the stability of heaven and earth: the Old Testament on the connection between creation and salvation.' Lohfink N. (ed.) *Theology of the Pentateuch*, Edinburgh: T. & T. Clark, 1994, 116–135.
7. May, G. *Creatio Ex Nihilo: the Doctrine of Creation out of Nothing in Early Christian Thought*. Edinburgh: T. & T. Clark, 1995.
8. Napier, B.D. 'On Creation-Faith in the Old Testament.' *Interpretation*, 1962, 16: 21–42.
9. Oeschlaeger, M. *Caring for Creation: an Ecumenical Approach to the Environmental Crisis*. New Haven: Yale University Press, 1994.
10. Thompson, P.E.S. 'The Yahwist Creation Story.' *Vetus Testamentum*, 1971, 21: 197–208.
11. van Bavel, T. 'The Creator and the integrity of creation in the Fathers of the Church.' *Augustinian Studies*, 1990, 21: 1–33.
12. DeWitt, C.B. 'Ecology and ethics: relation of religious belief to ecological practice in the Biblical tradition.' *Biodiversity and Conservation*, 1995, 4: 838–848.
13. White, L. 'The historical roots of our ecologic crisis.' *Science*, 1967, 155: 1203–1207.
14. Whitney, E. 'Lynn White, ecotheology and history.' *Environmental Ethics*, 1993, 15: 151–169.
15. Barr, J. 'The image of God in the Book of Genesis: a study of terminology.' *Bulletin of the John Rylands Library*, 1968, 51: 11–26.
16. Preuss, H.D. *Old Testament Theology*. Louisville, KY: Westminster John Knox Press, 1995.
17. Cohen, J. *'Be Fertile and Increase, Fill the Earth and Master It': The Ancient and Medieval Career of a Biblical Text*. Ithaca, NY: Cornell University Press, 1989.
18. Hall, D.J. *Imaging God: Dominion as Stewardship*. Grand Rapids: Eerdmans, 1986.
19. Cobb, J.B. *Sustainability: Economics, Ecology, and Justice*. Maryknoll: Orbis, 1992.
20. Nash, J. *Loving Nature: Ecological Integrity and Christian Responsibility*. Nashville: Abingdon, 1991.
21. Bauckham, R. Moltmann, Jürgen. In McGrath A.E. (ed.) *The Blackwell Encyclopaedia of Modern Christian Thought*, Oxford: Blackwell, 1993, 385–388.
22. Lewis, L.M. *The Promethean Politics of Milton, Blake and Shelley*. London: University of Missouri Press, 1992.
23. Trousson, R. *Le thème de Prométhée dans le literature européene*. Geneva: Droz, 1976.
24. Devereux, P., Steele, J. and Kubrin, D. *Earthmind: Communicating with the Living World of Gaia*. Rochester, VT: Destiny Books, 1989.
25. Ruether, R. *Gaia and God*. San Francisco: Harper & Row, 1989.

4 – Theology and ethics of the land

Chris Wright

The Revd Dr Chris Wright is Principal of All Nations College, Ware

Creation is not solely for human benefit – it has value in relation to God directly. There are a number of biblical concepts – for example, stewardship and servanthood, the land of Israel as a microcosm of the earth – which help us to explore what our attitude should be to God's creation.

Presented originally at a conference devoted to a Christian response to contemporary environmental issues,[1] this paper reflects that concern and is not aiming to provide a full account of the rich depths of biblical resources on the earth in general or the land of Israel in particular. An attempt to provide such a comprehensive synthesis can be found in my God's People in God's Land, which also gives wide bibliographical access to the work of other scholars in this field.[2]

Keywords: creation, ethics, land, redemption, Israel, Old Testament

God's earth: reflections from creation

Reflections on land obviously have to begin with the biblical theme of creation as it is found in the familiar texts of Genesis 1–11 and poetic texts such as Psalms 33, 104, etc. Considering the material with an ecological-ethical focus in mind, the following points seem significant.

The goodness of creation

This is one of the most obvious points of Genesis 1 and 2, in view of its repetition.[3] It sets the Hebrew account of creation in contrast to other Ancient Near Eastern accounts where powers and gods of the natural world are portrayed as having varying degrees of malevolence. Part of the meaning of the goodness of creation in the Bible is that it witnesses to the God who made it, reflecting something of his character. (e.g. Psalms 19, 29, 50:6, 65, 104, 148; Job 12:7–9; Acts 14:17; 17:27, Romans 1:20). That being the case, it is not going too far to make an analogy to the text 'He who oppresses the poor shows contempt for their Maker' (Proverbs 14:31, cf. 17:5), along the lines of 'He who destroys or degrades the earth dirties its reflection of its Maker'.

Creation, distinct and dependent

The affirmation that God created the heavens and the earth implies a fundamental ontological distinction between God as creator and everything created. This *duality* is essential to all biblical thought and to a Christian world view. It should not be confused with other kinds of unbiblical *dualism* (e.g. between body and soul). It stands against both monism and pantheism and thus is a major biblical point of contrast and polemic with New Age spirituality which adopts a broadly monistic world view.

The Bible not only denies the idea of ontological identity between the world and God, it also denies the idea that the world is a self-sustaining bio-system. The '*Gaia* hypothesis' as originally proposed by James E. Lovelock is a hypothesis about the interconnectedness of the whole biosphere.[4] Lovelock himself, while he suggested that the earth seems to behave like a single organism, a huge living creature, did not 'personalize' nature in the sense of regarding the whole biosphere as a divine being and indeed has rejected such religious metamorphoses of his work. But *Gaia* has certainly been taken that way in popular presentations of New Age thinking. The earth itself is regarded as god. The Bible, however, portrays the whole universe as separate from God and dependent on him for its existence and sustenance. This is not to deny that God has built into the earth an incredible capacity for renewal, recovery, balance, and adaptation. But the way in which all these systems work and interrelate is itself planned and sustained by God.[5]

The combination of these two points means that Christian ecological ethics need not be tarnished with some of the implicit or explicit pantheism of certain brands of 'Deep Green' ecology.[6] Evangelicals are easily repelled by the radical politics of some green advocates or the New Age links of others, and then fall into ecological indifference or conspiracy-hunting paranoia.[7] We need to oppose distortions not with negative apathy or hostility, but with the proper presentation of biblical truth.

Creation desacralised

The distinctness of creation from God not only rules out monism, it also ruled out nature polytheism, which was much more prevalent in the cultural and religious environment of Israel. Nature itself and natural forces were desacralised in the faith of Israel, that is, they had no intrinsic divine power. Thus, on the one hand, the fertility cults of Canaan were rejected, because Israel were taught that Yahweh himself provided the abundance of nature for them (e.g. Hosea 2:8ff.), and on the other hand, the immensely powerful and influential astral deities of Babylon were unmasked as nothing more than created objects under Yahweh's authority (Isaiah 40:26). In both cases, fertility and astrology, Israel's distinctive belief about creation brought them into severe cultural and political conflict with surrounding worldviews. The Hebrew Bible, therefore, while it can certainly be seen to inculcate respect and care for non-human creation, resists and reverses the human tendency to sacralise or personalise it, or to imbue it with any power independent of its personal Creator.[8]

Creation and humanity

It is not quite true to say that human beings were the climax of God's creation in Genesis 1–2. The real climax comes with God's own sabbath rest, as he entered into the enjoyment of his 'very good' creation. Yet even 'the sabbath was made for man', said Jesus. The sabbath day, as a recurrent reminder of the deeper 'rest' that was and remains God's purpose for creation as a whole, is for human benefit, and in that respect mirrors the rest of creation.

It is important to note that the creation is not *solely* for human benefit. The Old Testament gives it value in relation to God directly, to glorify him and to bring him delight. Creation is good and beautiful independently of our presence within it and our ability to observe it. This is at least part of the thrust of the speech of God in Job 38–39 with its majestic descriptions of created glories and curiosities, some of which are not even observed by humans, let alone for their benefit, at least directly (cf. 38:25ff.). It is also significant that in Genesis 1 the affirmation 'It is good' was not made by Adam and Eve in the creation narratives but by God himself. That is, the goodness of creation (which includes its beauty) is theologically and chronologically prior to human observation. It is something that God 'saw' before humanity was around to see it. So the goodness of creation is not merely a human reflexive response to a pleasant view on a sunny day. It is rather the seal of divine approval on the whole universe.

Missiologically there is an important point here too. If creation were exclusively for human benefit rather than being primarily for God's glory and pleasure, then active caring for creation could be accused of being just another form of human self-serving. Now of course it *is* true that in caring for creation we ultimately also do what is best for humanity, but the task has a legitimacy of its own as well. In serving the non-human created order we are also serving God and fulfilling a mandate never revoked.

However, it is clear that the Bible does recognize the uniqueness of human beings, both in the fact that they alone of all creatures have been made by God in his own image, and in the fact that God explicitly gives human beings a position of priority within creation (Genesis 1:29, 2:9ff.; Psalms 65:9,

104:15, etc.). Indeed, there is a view in science known as 'the anthropic principle', which suggests that in some sense the initial conditions at the very origin of the universe, on a Big Bang understanding of it, had to be very precisely set in order to produce the relatively recent conditions in which human life on planet earth has been possible, with its incredible potential for discovering what those initial conditions actually were.[9]

This principle need not be derided as the kind of anthropocentrism which gives us license to abuse, neglect, rape or destroy the natural environment. The accusations of Lynn White[10] and others may be justified to some extent as regards the arrogance of westernized Christian cultures towards creation, but they are not justified biblically.

On the other hand, it is a principle which does give biblical legitimacy to the priority of human beings within the created order. Rejected as 'speciesism' by some Deep Ecologists, this has to be maintained by Christian ethics, in relation both to environmental issues and the emotive question of animal rights. The uniqueness of human beings by virtue of their definitive nature as created in the image of God means that wherever a conflict exists between human needs and those of other animate or inanimate parts of creation – *a conflict which cannot be satisfactorily resolved by meeting the needs of both simultaneously* – then human beings take priority. This of course raises enormous issues of justice as well as environmental ethics, as the 'Earth Summit' in Rio de Janeiro in 1992 highlighted. From a Christian point of view, it is this principle which makes the conflict, in some contexts, between developmental and environmental objectives so sharp.

Servanthood

The word *Stewardship* stood as the heading of this section in the original draft, but has been changed in the light of points made at the conference.[1] 'Stewardship' is commonly used in Christian circles as a term implying appeals for money ('stewardship campaigns'), and is sometimes used in non-Christian circles to give a moral aura to what may be unscrupulous exploitation of resources. The term 'servanthood', on the other hand, reflects two biblical truths: first, that Christ, as Lord of Creation exercised his Lordship historically through becoming a servant, so dominion through servanthood is both biblical and Christlike; second, that God's instruction to the man he placed in the garden in Eden was literally 'to serve it and keep it' (Genesis 2:15).We humans have been given dominion over the rest of creation, but it is to be exercised by serving creation on God's behalf.

God entrusted the earth to human management (Genesis 1:28, 2:15) and has not revoked the trust deed, in spite of the mess we have made of it. The concept of 'dominion' has been misunderstood (as mentioned above), but biblically includes both responsibility for the earth itself and its non-human resources (cf. the concern for trees and animals in OT law, e.g. Deuteronomy 20:19f., 22:1–4,6, 25:4) and the exercise of justice in human economic relationships. Elsewhere, I have suggested four basic principles that are threaded through the economic understanding of stewardship (in its proper sense) in the Old Testament: (a) shared access to natural resources, in view of the fact that the earth was given to humanity as a whole; (b) the right and responsibility of productive work; (c) the expectation of growth and the naturalness of exchange and trade; and (d) justice in the sharing and use of the products of human effort.[11]

Earth under curse: the fall

The biblical description of the entrance of sin and evil into human life significantly includes its effect in the realm of the human relation to the earth, and particularly the soil. I do not wish to enter here into the debate as to whether the fall of humanity can be said to be responsible for all the phenomena in nature which we regard as threatening or catastrophic from our human point of view.[12] But the event described in Genesis

3 is certainly portrayed as having radically distorted and fractured our relationship with the earth itself, and also, as Paul points out (Romans 8:20f., echoing probably Ecclesiastes), as having frustrated the creation's function in relation to God. In my view, much Christian thinking about the earth does not take sufficient account of the biblical reality of God's curse upon it. Perhaps it is a sentimental discomfort with God being associated with anything 'not nice'. It is easier to lay all the blame on the devil. Perhaps it is lack of familiarity with Ecclesiastes . . .

Earth under covenant: Noah

Equally, however, much other Christian thinking about the earth far too readily jumps on the band-wagon of doom and gloom, as if the fate of the entire cosmos depended on which deodorant spray we use. That is to ignore the tremendous significance of the covenant with Noah. God has entered into a covenant commitment with all life on earth (explicitly not just human life, Genesis 8:21f., 9:8–17) to preserve the necessary conditions of life on the planet. How long he will continue to do so is not stated, except that it will be 'as long as the earth endures'. The point is that the future of the planet rests finally in God's hands, not ours. This is of course not meant to induce complacency or indifference to urgent environmental issues. I am not saying that as human beings we could not contrive to destroy much of the planet or to render it virtually uninhabitable. But such a catastrophe, if it ever takes place, will not be outside the sovereign will and power of God and his purpose in history. We live not only in a cursed earth, but also in a covenanted earth, and have to cope with the tension. It is tragic that the rainbow has been hijacked as a New Age symbol when it could and should be the symbol of positive, hope-filled Christian affirmation about our world.

Israel's land: reflections from redemption

Noah: prototype of new creation

Noah got his name (echoes of 'comfort' and 'rest') because of his father Lamech's longing for God to lift the curse from the earth (Genesis 5:29). This is a clue to the earliest biblical understanding of what salvation should mean. If the effect of sin was to blight and belabour human existence in the earth by laying it under curse, then this antediluvian longing points to the answer: let God remove his curse from the earth. Not, one notes, let us human beings escape to heaven somewhere, leaving the earth behind. The consistent biblical hope, from Genesis to Revelation is that God should do something with the earth so that we can once again dwell upon it in 'rest', with him. The Bible speaks predominantly of God coming here, not of us going somewhere else.

Lamech did not see the answer to the wish he made on Noah's birthday. On the biblical reckoning of the years, he missed it by five years and should have been glad to. For when it came, it was an act of simultaneous judgement and salvation which in *both* dimensions included the natural creation along with human beings. Theologically, the flood is a prototype of both sides of God's response to the cursed earth: destruction and renewal. An old sinful world perished. A new world began as Noah's family and his animal menagerie stepped out onto Mount Ararat. The echoes of the creation narrative are strong in Genesis 8:15–17. It was, of course, still the old world not yet washed clean of its sin, as the narrative quickly shows. But the whole story becomes the sign not only of God's commitment to life on earth while it lasts (in the covenant tied up with its rainbow ribbon), but also of the coming final judgement and renewal – the new creation (cf. 2 Peter 3).

The covenant with Abraham: land as an integral part of redemptive blessing

It is not surprising, therefore, that the covenant promise which actually launched the work of redemption in history included land in its terms. In fact in purely statistical terms, land is clearly the dominant note in the ancestral promise. Out of 46 references to the promise in Genesis to Judges, only seven do not mention the land while 29 refer solely to it (e.g. in Genesis 28:4, the 'blessing of Abraham' is simply possession of the land).[13]

There is thus a continuity and consistency in the total biblical story. Genesis 1–11 shows humanity in God's earth, but living in a state of alienation from it and longing for restoration and the removal of the curse from the land. The concluding vision of Scripture looks to a new creation in which God will once again dwell with redeemed humanity. The foundational redemptive covenant of grace with Abraham, therefore, includes land in order to make particular and local what will ultimately be universal – blessing not only to all nations but also to the whole earth itself.

Israel's land as microcosm of the earth

It follows from the above point that Canaan, as the land of Israel, has to be viewed in the light of the universality of the Abraham covenant as well as its particularity. That is, while the historical gift of the land to the tribes of Israel is certainly described in the Old Testament as the direct action of God in faithfulness to his promise to Abraham, that promise had as its ultimate scope the blessing of all nations. Its other two main ingredients have that in view: posterity (the fact that Abraham would become a nation, which would be the vehicle of God's blessing to the nations) and relationship (the special covenant relationship between God and Israel, which the Old Testament envisages being ultimately extended to the nations). The land element has to be viewed consistently in the same universal context. Israel possessed its land as part of its mission in relation to the rest of the nations and as part of God's redemptive intention for the whole earth. That is a vitally important point concerning the concept of election.

This link between the land of Israel and the whole earth can be viewed eschatologically, as we shall note below, but, as we have already seen, it is also vitally important as the basis for a *paradigmatic* understanding of the relevance of Old Testament Israel to other cultures and societies separated by history and geography. Israel was created and commissioned to be 'a light to the nations'. There was, therefore, a sense in which everything connected with them was exemplary in principle. The gifts of land to live in and law to live by were intrinsic to the way God shaped Israel to be a 'model' people. All the time one studies the particulars of Israel's social, economic and political structures one must keep in mind the universal goal of their existence in the first place. This important hermeneutical principle helps to unlock the relevance of the Old Testament for our own ethical construction in many areas, including especially ecological concern.[14]

Among the clearest parallels between creation teaching about the whole earth and Israel's theology of their land are the twin themes of divine ownership and divine gift. The creation basis of OT teaching gives us two complementary truths about the earth: on the one hand, it belongs to God who made it (Psalms 24:1, 89:11, 95:4f.; Jeremiah 27:4ff.; 1 Chronicles 29:11); on the other hand, it has been given and entrusted to human beings (Psalms 115:16, 8:6; Genesis 1:28–30). God, as ultimate owner, thus retains the right of moral control over how the earth is used. As we saw above, human beings, as stewards and 'servant-managers', are accountable to God for the care and use of the earth and all its resources.

Israel's system of land tenure embodied the same two principles. On the one hand, the land was God's gift to Israel, an essential part of the promise to Abraham and a tangible proof of his faithfulness. As their 'inheritance', it was at the heart of their covenant relationship to Yahweh. On the other hand, the land was still owned by God (Leviticus 25:23), so that as divine landlord he retained authority over how it should be used. Hence Israel's whole economic system was subject to God's moral critique. The paradigmatic connection between Israel as a society and the rest of humanity means that we can make positive use of Israel's comprehensive and detailed laws and institutions concerning the distribution and use of land in our own efforts to think biblically about economic and environmental ethics in our day. This gives us a broader and richer set of resources, with a greater degree of practical specificity and sharpness, than the application of the creation principle of stewardship alone. While fundamental and challenging, that principle is higher up the 'ladder of abstraction', whereas the specific land economics of Israel are at ground level.

Creation values in redeemed economics

When we turn to examine the details of Israel's economic legislation, it is possible to see how much of it was geared to restoring the creation values referred to above. In a fallen world, such a restoration cannot be total, so one finds the same kind of tension in OT economics between the ideal and the given reality that is also there in other aspects of OT law and ethics (e.g. on divorce, slavery, etc.). Thus, taking up each of the four principles referred to earlier:[15]

(a) Shared access to and use of the land and its resources were built into the initial distribution of the land among the tribes at the time of the settlement. The purpose was made very clear – that each tribe, clan and family should have sufficient according to its size and needs (Numbers 26:52–56; Joshua 13–19).

(b) The right and responsibility of productive work are reflected in the sizeable number of laws concerning working humans and animals, slaves, hired labour, conditions of work, treatment by employers, payment, sabbath and festival rest, etc. (e.g. Exodus 21:1–6, 20f., 26f.; Job 31:14; Leviticus 25:39f., 43, 19:13; Deuteronomy 24:14f.; Jeremiah 22:13; Exodus 20:11, 23:12; Isaiah 58:3–14; Deuteronomy 25:4).

(c) Economic growth in material goods and provisions is both validated and put under careful control and critique, from the tenth commandment ('You shall not covet') onwards. The same chapter of Deuteronomy points to the God-given goal of abundance and sufficiency (8:7–10), and the dangers of excessive surplus (8:11–18). Most interestingly, and of great practical effect in Israel throughout its whole biblical history as far as the evidence shows, was the principle of inalienability of family land. Land itself was not to be treated as a commercial commodity, for private speculation and profit. It could not be bought or sold, apart from within the kinship groups (Leviticus 25:23ff.). The story of Naboth (1 Kings 21) and its context shows that the violation of this principle involved a capitulation to a foreign religious world-view on the one hand and the invasion of gross rural injustice on the other.

(d) Justice in the use and distribution of the products of economic activity is also a major concern of OT law. There can be all kinds of 'neutral' reasons why some people become wealthier and others poorer.[16] The OT law seeks to redress the economic balance by structural measures aimed especially at the control of debt (Exodus 22:25; Leviticus 25:36f.; Deuteronomy 23:19f., 24:6,10) and other tactics to relieve poverty and to restore the poor to dignified participation in the community – gleaning rights (Leviticus 19:9f.; Deuteronomy 24:19–22), storage and distribution of the triennial tithe (Deuteronomy 14:22–27, 26:12ff.), the sabbatical year (Exodus 23:11; Leviticus 25:6f.; Deuteronomy 15:1–3), the jubilee year (Leviticus 25:8ff.), etc. All of this was part of the structures of Israel's economic system, to encourage justice and compassion in the ordinary vicissitudes of a functioning economy.[17] This is not yet even to mention the reaction of the Old Testament to poverty and injustice caused by direct oppression and greed – i.e. the economic message of the prophets.

The link between human morality and ecological health

The land functioned like a moral and spiritual barometer in the Old Testament. So much of the prophetic anger is directed at economic injustice and oppression, in which the abuse and misuse of the land is dominant. On the one hand, Israel fell into the kind of nature polytheism that characterized the Canaanite view of the land, and thus compromised their unique covenant relationship with Yahweh. On the other hand, they allowed economic practices in the use of land, mostly associated with the monarchy, which eventually polarized the nation into a wealthy land-owning elite and an oppressed peasant population. In other words, the land stood at the junction of the vertical and the horizontal covenant relationships. The combination of idolatry and injustice is still much in evidence in our own world, provided we are careful and comprehensive in our evaluation of what constitutes each of these.

Sometimes the specifically ecological aspect is brought into focus. Psalm 72, for example, positively looks for environmental and economic well-being as a by-product of just and benevolent government. Conversely, Hosea 4:1–3 climaxes the list of social evils with the observation that nature itself is suffering the consequences (I think the text is going further than a mere personification of nature in response to a broken covenant). Habakkuk 2, in the midst of a series of woes against the Babylonian excesses, includes gross environmental damage along with the normal victims of war.

> The violence you have done to Lebanon will
>   overwhelm you,
> and your destruction of animals will terrify you.
> For you have shed man's blood;

> you have destroyed lands and cities and everyone in them
> (Habakkuk 2:17; 'Lebanon' is almost certainly a figure for forests, as the parallel with 'animals' suggests.)

The American deforestation of vast areas of Vietnam in the course of the Vietnam war, and the Iraqi ecological atrocities in the Gulf in the Gulf War give the ancient prophetic text a chilling relevance.[18]

Jesus affirmed the goodness of creation and demonstrated his lordship over it

Turning all too briefly to the NT,[19] we have to begin with the tremendous fact that the incarnation itself affirmed and vindicated the goodness of creation. From there we could take note of the highly positive attitude of Jesus to nature, both in his direct teaching and in his parables (e.g. Matthew 6:26ff., 10:29, etc.). And as scholars have often pointed out, his miracles of calming the storm and walking on the sea demonstrate not merely the power of the creator, but specifically that power in relation to the element of creation normally associated in OT thought with the chaotic, uncontrollable forces of nature – the sea. Hence the astonished question of his disciples (Matthew 8:27).

The atonement and resurrection include creation in their effects

Paul affirms that through the atoning death of Jesus on the cross, 'all things' in creation have been reconciled to God (Colossians 1:20). The scope of Christ's redeeming work is thus as universal as the scope of his creating and sustaining work already referred to (Colossians 1:16f.). Likewise, the resurrection is not only the vindication of the whole created order,[20] but is also the first-fruits of a new creation.

New Creation: reflections from eschatology

Return to land symbolic of restored relationship

Having jumped ahead to NT eschatology, we must pause to step back to the OT. As the prophets spoke about the devastating loss of land that came upon Israel in the early 6th century BC, and then enabled Israel to see beyond it to a restored relationship with God, it was the land itself that stood at the fulcrum of their message.[21] Thus, in Jeremiah 30-34, Isaiah 40-55 and Ezekiel 36-48, to name just the major text blocks, the promised restoration of Israel after the time of judgement is expressed in terms of return to the land. There are many new dimensions to this fresh promise, but it never 'evaporates' into the spiritual stratosphere. Land was still part of God's redemptive package for Israel in the centuries before Christ.

Future blessing portrayed as a super-abundance of nature

However, one feature of these and other texts (e.g. Amos 9:13-15) is the vision not merely of a return to the land as it was (that in fact turned out to be a tough new assignment for the tiny post-exilic restoration community, fraught with many disappointments), but of a renewed nature, echoing Eden itself in abundance and beauty. In other words, as Israel's eschatology sought to express its conception of God's ultimate purposes, it found its most natural resource in God's original purpose – namely a good and perfect earth available for human enjoyment and blessing.

The final vision: a new creation

The climax of Old Testament eschatological vision regarding creation is found in Isaiah 65-66. The words, 'Behold, I am creating new heavens and a new earth' (Isaiah 65:17), introduce a wonderful section which portrays God's new world as a place which is joyful, life-fulfilling, with guaranteed work satisfaction, and environmentally safe! It is a vision that puts most New Age dreams in the shade. This, and related passages are the scriptural (OT) foundation for the NT hope, which, far from rejecting or denying the earth as such or envisaging us floating off to some place else, looks forward likewise to a new, redeemed creation (Romans 8:18ff.), in which righteousness will dwell after purging judgement (2 Peter 3:10–13[22]) because God himself will dwell there with his people (Revelation 21:1–4).

The ecological relevance of biblical eschatology

Finally, as Francis Bridger points out, the eschatological orientation of all biblical ethics has the important consequence of protecting our ecological concern from becoming either purely anthropocentric or pantheistically earth-centred.

> 'The primary argument for ecological responsibility lies in the connection between old and new creation ... We are called to be stewards of the earth by virtue not simply of our orientation to the Edenic command of the Creator but also because of our orientation to the future. In acting to preserve and enhance the created order we are pointing to the coming rule of God in Christ ... Ecological ethics are not, therefore, anthropocentric: they testify to the vindicating acts of God in creation and redemption ... Paradoxically, the fact that it is God who will bring about a new order of creation at the End and that we are merely erecting signposts to that future need not act as a disincentive. Rather it frees us from the burden of ethical and technological autonomy and makes it clear that human claims to sovereignty are relative. The knowledge that it is God's world, that our efforts are not directed toward the construction of an ideal utopia but that we are, under God, building bridge-heads of the kingdom serves to humble us and to bring us to the place of ethical obedience.'[23]

We might finish, however, with a poem more in the genre of the prophets and psalmists.

> The time of rest, the promised Sabbath comes! ...
> Rivers of gladness water all the earth,
> And clothe all climes with beauty. The reproach
> Of barrenness is past. The fruitful field

Laughs with abundance; and the land, once lean
Or fertile only in its own disgrace,
Exults to see its thistly curse repeal'd.
The various seasons woven into one,
And that one season an eternal spring,
The garden fears no blight, and needs no fence,
For there is none to covet, all are full.
The lion, and the lizzard, and the bear
Graze with the fearless flocks ...
One song employs all nations, and all cry,
"Worthy the Lamb, for He was slain for us!"
The dwellers in the vales and on the rocks
Shout to each other, and the mountain tops
From distant mountains catch the flying joy,
Till, nation after nation taught the strain,
Earth rolls the rapturous Hosanna round.
(William Cowper, *The Task*, Book 6, lines 733, 763–744, 791–797)

Notes

1. This paper was first presented at the WEF conference on Ethics and the Environment in September 1992 at the Au Sable Institute, Michigan, USA, and subsequently published as 'Biblical reflections on land' in *Evangelical Review of Theology*, 1993, 17: 153–167.
2. Still probably the most thorough and stimulating monograph on this theme is the seminal work of Brueggeman, W. *The Land*, Philadelphia: Fortress, 1977.
3. Ron Elsdon makes the theme of the goodness of creation the thread running through his survey of biblical material in both testaments on this issue in his book, *Green House Theology: Biblical Perspectives on Caring for Creation*, Tunbridge Wells: Monarch, 1992.
4. Lovelock, J. *Gaia: A New Look at Life on Earth*, Oxford: Oxford University Press, 1979. For a survey and critique of New Age ecological views and their influence on recent Christian thought, see Wilkinson, L. (ed.) *Earthkeeping in the Nineties: Stewardship of Creation*, Grand Rapids: Eerdmans, revised edition, 1991, 181–199, and *idem.*, 'New age, new consciousness and the new creation', in Granberg-Michaelson, W. (ed.) *Tending the Garden: Essays on the Gospel and the Earth*, Grand Rapids: Eerdmans, 1987, 6–29.
5. I have immensely enjoyed reading Gleick, J. *Chaos: Making a New Science*, Penguin, 1987, with its fascinating account of the mysteries of living and dynamic systems, inorganic, organic and human, and the progress being made in understanding some of their inner simplicities. Gleick refers in passing to Lovelock's hypothesis, but his book is not interested in the religious or philosophical aspects of its topic, but is a historical and descriptive account of 'chaos theory' in several branches of science.
6. Cf. Bishop, S. 'Green theology and deep ecology: New Age or new creation?' *Themelios*, 1991, 16.3, 8–14.
7. Cf. Cumbey, C. *The Hidden Dangers of the Rainbow: The New Age Movement and Our Coming Age of Barbarism*, Shreveport, La.: Huntingdon House, 1983, and Hunt, D. *Peace, Prosperity and the Coming Holocaust*, Eugene, Oregon: Harvest House, 1983.

8. It is important to distinguish between *personalising* and *personifying* nature. The Old Testament frequently personifies nature as a rhetorical device, a figure of speech, for greater effect. For example, the heavens and earth are summoned to bear witness to God's address to his people (e.g. Deuteronomy 30:19, 32:1; Isaiah 1:2; Psalm 50:1–6), they declare his glory (Psalm 19), they rejoice at his judgement (Psalms 96:11–13, 98:7–9). Most vividly, the land itself 'vomited out' the previous inhabitants for their wickedness, and did the same to the Israelites when they followed suit (Leviticus 18:25–28). But the point of this rhetorical personification of nature is to underline either the personal character of the God who created it and is active in and through it, or to express the personal and moral nature of human beings' relationship to God. It is not ascribing personhood to nature or natural forces in themselves. In fact, to *personalise* nature in that way results in both *de*personalising God and *de*-moralising the relationship between humanity and God. To accord to creation the *personal* status and honour that is due only to God (or derivatively to humans who bear his image) is a form of idolatry as ancient as the fall itself (cf. Romans 1:21–25), though now given new characteristically twentieth century dress in the New Age movements.
9. Stephen Hawking discusses various versions of the anthropic principle (though he disagrees with them) in *A Brief History of Time*, London: Bantam Press, 1988, 124ff. Simply put, the principle is saying that this universe *had* to be as it is and has been since the beginning for creatures such as ourselves to emerge. It is a non-theological, non-purposive way of expressing the theological affirmation that the universe was created *for the purpose* of the arrival of humanity within it.
10. White, L. 'The historical roots of our ecologic crisis.' *Science*, 1967, 155, 1203–1207.
11. See *Living as the People of God (An Eye for an Eye)*, IVP, 1983, chapter 4.
12. This is a deep and complex issue, which the conference itself was not able to resolve. One question is whether the curse on the earth is ontological (i.e. affects the very nature of the cosmos as it now is), or functional (i.e. affecting only our human moral relationship with the earth and with God). The former view allows its adherents to attribute destructive natural phenomena such as earthquakes to the curse, though the chronological problem remains that the natural causes of such events long pre-date the arrival of the human species. Another question is whether features of nature
which we as human beings find 'unpleasant', such as carnivorous species, are the result of the fall or were always part of 'the way things were' long before humans existed let alone sinned. Cf. the response to Stephen Bishop's article by Michael Roberts in *Themelios*, 1991, 17.1: 16.
13. A detailed survey of the material is given by von Rad, G. 'The Promised Land and Yahweh's Land in the Hexateuch' in *The Problem of the Hexateuch and Other Essays*, London: SCM, 1966, and Philadelphia: Fortress, 1984, 79–93.
14. For further elaboration of what is meant by a paradigmatic approach to OT ethics, see my *Living as the People of God (An Eye for an Eye)*.
15. Detailed discussion of the points following will be found in *Living as the People of God (An Eye for an Eye)*, 76–87. For a fuller and more technical study of Israel's economic system, cf. my *God's People in God's Land: Family, Land and Property in the Old Testament*, Eerdmans/Paternoster, 1990. Israel's economic history has received several specific investigations recently, including Dearman, J.A. *Property Rights in the Eighth-Century Prophets: The Conflict and its Background*, Atlanta: Scholars, 1988; Gnuse, R. *You Shall Not Steal: Community and Property in the Biblical Tradition*, Maryknoll: Orbis, 1985.
16. These may include harsh climatic conditions in one place, differences of soil fertility, lack of children, illness, effects of war in border regions, etc. The point is, poverty is not necessarily the result of injustice and oppression by the rich, even though that is the major reason highlighted by the prophets. The economic laws of Israel, however, were concerned to redress impoverishment, regardless of its causes.

17. A very thorough survey of this material is provided by John Mason in Biblical teaching and assisting the poor', *Transformation*, 1987, 4.2: 1–14.
18. Elsdon, R. *Green House Theology: Biblical Perspectives on Caring for Creation*, Tunbridge Wells: Monarch, 1992, 102–107, gives some staggering statistics in relation to these two wars alone, in a book which is an excellent survey of the subject.
19. The inadequacy of this NT section of the paper can be rectified by the excellent symposium edited by DeWitt, C. *The Environment and the Christian: What Can We Learn from the New Testament?* Grand Rapids: Baker, 1991.
20. This is a point strongly developed by Oliver O'Donovan in *Resurrection and Moral Order*, Leicester: IVP, 1986; 2nd edn Apollos, 1994.
21. Still the best survey of this whole theme, with constant suggestive attention to its contemporary relevance, is Brueggemann, W. *The Land*, Philadelphia, Fortress, 1977. Various aspects of the issue are also explored in my *God's People in God's Land*, Grand Rapids: Eerdmans, 1990.
22. At the end of 2 Peter 3:10, I prefer the textual reading that the earth 'will be found' to the emendation reflected in several English translations 'will be burned up'. I also find Bauckham's interpretation of this convincing, namely that the earth will be 'found out', i.e., exposed and laid bare (cf. *NIV*) before God's judgement so that the wicked and all their works will no longer be able to hide or find any protection. (Bauckham, B.J. *Jude, 2 Peter*, Word Biblical Commentary, Waco: Word, 1983, 316–322. The purpose of the conflagration described in these verses is not the destruction of the cosmos *per se, but rather its purging and new creation.*
23. Bridger, F. 'Ecology and eschatology: a neglected dimension.' *Tyndale Bulletin*, 1990, 41.2: 290–301. This article was a response and addition to an earlier one by Hay D.A. 'Christians in the Global Greenhouse.' *Tyndale Bulletin*, 1990, 41.1: 109–127.

5 – The Old Testament and the environment: A response to Chris Wright

Gordon Wenham

> Gordon Wenham is Professor in Religious Studies at the Cheltenham & Gloucester College of Higher Education
>
> The life of an ancient Israelite was intimately tied to the natural environment, whereas modern urban dwellers are largely cocooned from it. Biblical reasons for human beings' obligations to God's creation are given.
>
> **Keywords:** environment, Old Testament, animals, plants, animal welfare, dominion

Introduction

When we talk of the environment today we are not simply talking about the surface of the earth as a piece of real estate, some of which was assigned to ancient Israel and therefore invested with special significance. Environmental issues concern the resources we draw from the land, the plants that grow on the land, the living creatures that inhabit the earth and man's relationship with them all. Chris Wright makes some passing reference to these issues but I am sure we would like biblical theologians to say more.

Strangely books on Old Testament theology[1] and ethics say hardly anything on these topics, at least if one relies on their indices. Yet it has been observed that animals are mentioned on nearly every one of the thousand pages of the Old Testament. This is not surprising, for Old Testament people were intimately involved in the environment throughout life. The weather determined whether their crops would flourish or fail. They drew water from the local well. They depended on animals to plough their fields, transport their goods, for clothing, for food and for sacrifice. Often some of them lived in the courtyard of their houses. Yet though Old Testament people were much closer to nature than we are, they also perceived nature as potentially more hostile. They could be killed by lions or bears. If drought did not cause famine, locusts or disease could be equally fatal.

By contrast modern urban dwellers are largely cocooned from the environment. We live in solid centrally heated houses supplied by well organised utility companies, depend on machines for transport, food and clothing production, and never feel threatened by other kinds of life except perhaps bacteria and viruses. Whereas in ancient times people lived in daily contact with the natural world, Westerners today only encounter it through TV or tourism or in vestigial form such as pets and gardening. But these are mere hobbies, optional extras not vital activities for human survival as they once were for nearly everyone.

Thus to understand what the Old Testament says about the environment we must first project ourselves back into the lifestyle of the Bible writers. Many comments in the Old Testament simply illustrate their situation, and are hardly normative. However, second, there are texts in the Old Testament that clearly theorise about the environment, about plants, animals, and their relationship to humans and God. These theoretical texts must therefore be explored before, third, we move on to discuss the ethical comments which indicate how the Old Testament expected ancient Israelites to treat natural resources, plant and animal life. Finally, after this essentially descriptive exercise we come to the most difficult and controversial stage, that of assessing the relevance of biblical ideas to our very different world and applying them where appropriate. It is at this point that my expertise in Old Testament reaches the end of its usefulness and the knowledge and skills of others become indispensable. So I shall end my paper by asking some questions.

My paper thus falls into four unequal parts, which I have entitled: (1) the life of an ancient Israelite, (2) humans' relationship to their God-given environment, (3) humans' obligations towards the environment, and (4) the hermeneutical issue: does the Old Testament speak to today's debate?

1. The life of an ancient Israelite

Numerous historical, archaeological and geographical studies[2] as well as careful reading of the Old Testament text have given us a clear view of the lifestyle of ordinary Israelites in the period in which most of the texts were written roughly 1200–500 BC. The Israelite heartland, the hills of Judah and Samaria, would still have been heavily wooded when the Israelite tribes first settled there. They built their typical four-roomed houses round a courtyard and farmed the land around them. When the children grew up, the daughters married out but the sons stayed on the family estate, which they tried to enlarge by cutting down more trees. Apart from a few merchants, skilled workers, and those employed in the court, most people depended on their land and animals for survival. Figs, vines, and olives were grown on the terraced hills. Some grain would also have been planted on the terraces, and more in the valleys. Most families would have owned flocks of goats and sheep, which doubtless roamed far and wide looking for pasture. The most valuable animals were cattle which served as tractors as well as producing milk, meat and hides.

By and large the Old Testament paints a rosy picture of life in the land. Canaan is a land 'flowing with milk and honey'. Unlike Egypt which depended on human irrigation with the foot, Canaan is fed by rain from heaven (Deuteronomy 11:11), and the grapes grow in clusters so huge that they need two men to carry them (Numbers 13:23). The patriarchs' flocks flourished in the land (Genesis 26:14), while the Psalmist rejoices that the 'valleys stand so thick with corn that they shall laugh and sing' (Psalm 65:14).

But it was a precarious existence. Though the average winter rainfall of Israel is adequate (20 inches or more), it is variable in its timing and quantity. If it started late or ended early, crops would be poor, and if there was too little rain, there would be famine affecting both people and animals (Jeremiah 14:2–6). Without deep wells and sprinklers nothing humanly could be done to remedy the situation. Prayer, emigration or death were the only options when stores ran out (Genesis 12:10; Ruth 1:1).

Drought was not the only threat to life though. The woods were home in Bible times to numerous wild animals, such as lions and bears, which could kill humans and their livestock (1 Samuel 17:34). Survival could also be threatened by plagues of insects, such as locusts, or crop diseases (Deuteronomy 28:22,39,42). Although Mesopotamians felt threatened by overpopulation, ancient Israel was concerned that for lack of energetic workers they would not be able to keep the wildlife at bay (Exodus 23:29) or prevent the cultivated vine terraces being overrun by briars and thistles (Proverbs 24:30–34; Isaiah 7:23).

The biblical writers were therefore fully involved with the natural environment. They knew at first hand the joys and problems of ancient Israelite agriculture. They recognised the natural fertility of the land given them by God, and saw this as one of his great blessings to them. But on the other hand they were well aware that their existence in the land could not be taken for granted: God could withhold the rain and that would bring national disaster, or mere sloth could bring personal ruin as the weeds gained the upper hand.

2. Humans' relationship to the environment

Water and other natural resources

This ambivalent situation is reflected in the texts that discuss the theology of the environment. Little is said about natural resources except water. Canaan is a 'land of brooks of water, of fountains and springs, flowing forth in valleys and hills ... a land whose stones are iron, and out of whose hills you can dig copper'[3] (Deuteronomy 8:7–9). Deuteronomy expects these resources to be enjoyed thankfully: 'you shall bless the LORD your God for the good land he has given you' (8:10).

Deuteronomy's description of Canaan's bounty echoes the description of Eden in Genesis in which a large river flowed dividing into four branches presumably watering the many trees that it featured. Eden also contained gold and precious stones. Ezekiel also draws on this picture of Eden when he describes the new temple as having a river flowing out of it eastwards down the Kedron valley to the Dead Sea. 'When it enters the stagnant waters of the sea, the water will become fresh. And wherever the river goes every living creature which swarms will live, and there will be very many fish ... And on the banks, on both sides of the river, there will grow all kinds of trees for food. Their leaves will not wither nor their fruit fail, but they will bear fresh fruit every month, because the water for them flows from the sanctuary' (Ezekiel 47:8–12).

Within the Bible water is often a symbol for the life-giving power of God, but in the hot dry climate of the Middle East it also inescapably reflects reality. Without water everything quickly dies.

Plants

Whereas earth's natural resources are largely a topic for wonder and grateful appropriation (e.g. Job 36:27–38:38; Psalm 104), much more is said about plant life, its place in God's plan, and people's relationship to it. The account of creation in Genesis 1 climaxes with the creation of humans on the sixth day and in a sense all the work of the previous days prepares for this. Day three with the emergence of the dry land from the universal ocean and the growth of the first plants is a large step in preparing a habitable environment for human life. Two main kinds of vegetation are distinguished, plants and trees. Both are characterised by bearing seed and propagating themselves according to their kind. The repeated references to seed bearing and kinds of vegetation hint at God's concern that life should continue and affirm that the different types of plant life are organised by him.

The relevance of plants to human existence becomes explicit on day six after the creation of land animals and humans. Plants and trees bearing seed are assigned to humans to eat, whereas other plants are given to the animals to eat. The reason for the distinction is not very clear, but basically humans are assigned fruits and grain, whereas the animals are expected to eat grass and leaves. Both animals and humans are here portrayed as originally all vegetarians, an idea that was widespread in ancient cultures. It is also striking that whereas in Babylonian thinking humanity was created to provide the gods with food, in Genesis God provides food for humans.

The idea that God provides fruit trees to feed humans is the starting point of the garden of Eden story. As soon as Adam has been placed in the garden 'the LORD God made to grow every tree that is pleasant to the sight and good for food'. Adam is then told he may freely eat of every tree save one. In this way Genesis stresses God's bountiful provision for human need: in the beginning human beings enjoyed a more than adequate supply of high-quality food with minimum effort.

However Adam and Eve's decision to eat the one forbidden fruit led to a complete change in their situation. Fig leaves are used to cover their nakedness and they hide from God among the trees – a comic situation were its longer-term consequences not so tragic, for Adam and Eve are punished by expulsion from this rich orchard to labour on the land to grow their own food. The curse on the ground describes humanity's plight ever since:

> 'Cursed is the ground because of you
> in toil you shall eat of it all the days of
>   your life;
> thorns and thistles it shall bring forth to
>   you;

and you shall eat the plants of the field.
In the sweat of your face you shall eat
bread' (Genesis 3:17–19).

In other words the difficulties faced by Israelite farmers go back to the first humans disobeying God's only command to them: 'Do not eat of that tree'. Disobedience to God's command is thus the root cause of human problems in food production.

The law and the prophets continually hammer home the message that obedience to the law will ensure plentiful rains and good harvests, while disobedience will result in drought and other agricultural disasters. 'If you ... observe my commandments ... I will give you your rains in their season, and the land shall yield its increase, and the trees of the field shall yield their fruit.' 'If you will not hearken to me ... I will make your heavens like iron and your earth like brass; and your strength shall be spent in vain, for your land shall not yield its increase' (Leviticus 26:3–4,18–20).

The fall profoundly affected eating patterns in another way. Genesis 3 is just the beginning of what has been termed an avalanche of sin. Adam and Eve's sin is followed by Cain's murder of his brother, Lamech's seventy-sevenfold vengeance, and universal violence by humans and animals ('all flesh') fills the earth, so that God decides to 'make an end of all flesh'. The flood follows, destroying everyone save Noah's family and pairs of every living creature. Genesis implies that the pre-flood violence does not just affect human beings but animals too, so that they attack each other and people as well. But Noah's sacrifice changes God's attitude to the endemic sinfulness and violence fundamentally, so that he makes a covenant with all flesh never to destroy the earth again in a flood. He also permits meat-eating with safeguards to underline the preciousness of life. Humans may eat meat, as long as they avoid consuming the blood, for that is its life (Genesis 8:20–9:5).

In this way Genesis explains the situation that faced the peasant farmers of ancient Palestine. Good crops are God's gifts to an obedient people whereas crop failure is a mark of God's anger at human sin. It is the primeval sin of Adam that explains the difficulties faced by the ancient Israelite farmer. But this does not exhaust Old Testament thought about the significance of plants. Strong flourishing trees were admired, and often the righteous are compared to them (Psalm 1:3; 52:8; 92:12–14). In particular the vine is often a symbol of Israel (Psalm 80:8–16; Isaiah 5:1–7). It also appears that wheat may also symbolise Israel or its tribes (Leviticus 24:5–6). It is striking that these highly valued foodstuffs which are also used in sacrifice may be identified with the chosen people: something similar happens with clean animals, i.e. those which may be eaten and often sacrificed, which also clearly symbolise Israel. The relationship between people and plants is not so intimate as that between animals and people, but these parallels do suggest there is a relationship even if weak between human and plant life, so that Isaiah can say 'All flesh is grass ... surely the people is grass' (40:6–7).

The law looks forward to a day when the nation will be so obedient that it will fully enjoy God's blessings, that the harvests will be so huge that they will not have finished gathering in one before the next is ready. 'Your threshing shall last to the time of vintage, and the vintage shall last to the time of sowing' (Leviticus 26:5). This hope becomes even brighter in the eschatological vision of the prophets. They look for the restoration to the prosperity of Eden

> 'The days are coming' says the LORD,
> 'when the ploughman shall overtake the reaper
> and the treader of grapes him who sows the seed;
> the mountains shall drip sweet wine,
> and all the hills shall flow with it'
> (Amos 9:13).
> Isaiah looks forward to a day when:
> The wilderness and dry land shall be glad,
> the desert shall rejoice and blossom
> like the crocus it shall blossom abundantly
> (35:1–2).

We have already looked at Ezekiel's vision of the new Jerusalem from which flows a huge river into the desert and makes the Dead Sea fresh (47:1–12). Thus in powerful images the prophets picture the perfecting of the environment so that it returns to the original peace and abundance that characterised creation at the beginning.

Animals

A similar pattern characterises the prophets' handling of the animal world. It was obvious to the ancients that humans are much closer to the animals than any other part of creation, and Genesis while affirming this closeness also defines the differences between humans and animals quite carefully. For example birds, fishes, animals and humans are all termed 'living creatures' (*nephesh hayyah*). Birds and fishes, like humans, are 'created' (a term used sparingly in Genesis 1 for the more dramatic stages of the creative process), they are all blessed by God, and commanded to be fruitful and multiply.[4] But only humans are said to be made in God's image. 'So God created man in his own image, in the image of God he created him; male and female he created them.' It is because humans alone are made in the divine image that they are given dominion over the rest of creation, a highly controversial topic in the environmental debate, so we shall pause and try and unpack Genesis' understanding of humanity's status here.

What constitutes the image of God has perplexed exegetes and theologians for centuries. It is something that distinguishes humans from the animals and links them with God and the angels, so all sorts of human characteristics, rationality, speech, moral and spiritual powers, have been identified with the divine image. While there may be truth in many of these suggestions, we cannot be sure.[5] More help comes from ancient Near Eastern sources. In both Egypt and Babylon the king was often regarded as God's image, that is his representative on earth ruling on his behalf. While this does not explain the essence of the image, it certainly clarifies its function. Because humans are made in God's image, they represent God on earth and rule for him. Making humans in God's image and giving them responsibility for the rest of creation are closely connected in Genesis 1:26: 'Let us make man in our image, after our likeness; and let them have dominion over the fish ... birds ... cattle and over all the earth'.

Psalm 8 puts the same ideas more explicitly and poetically:

> What is man that thou are mindful of him ... ?
> Yet thou hast made him little less than God,
> and dost crown him with glory and honour.
> Thou hast given him dominion over the works of thy hands;
> thou hast put all things under his feet,
> all sheep and oxen,
> and also the beasts of the field (Psalm 8:4–7).

Where the Bible differs from Egypt and Mesopotamia is in affirming that every human being, male and female, not just the king is made in God's image. This means that every human life is sacred and must be protected (Genesis 9:6). It also means that every human being is given authority over and responsibility for the rest of creation to manage it in the way that God would.

Two terms are used in Genesis to describe humans' management function vis-à-vis the rest of creation. They are told to 'have dominion' (Hebrew *radah*) over other living creatures, fish, birds, cattle and creeping things and to 'subdue' (*kabash*) the earth. 'Have dominion' is quite a positive term for ruling. Whereas many people today have an anarchist streak, or at least an antipathy to those in authority, that was not the official outlook of the ancient Near East, who saw kings as essentially benevolent and concerned with their subjects' welfare. Psalm 72 puts this message powerfully:

> Give the king thy justice, O God,
> May he judge thy people with righteousness
> and thy poor with justice!

Let the mountains bear prosperity for the
   people,
and the hills, in righteousness!
May he defend the cause of the poor of
   the people,
give deliverance to the needy,
and crush the oppressor! (Psalm
72:1–3)

To 'have dominion' means to be in charge of something, e.g. workers (1 Kings 4:24; 9:23). To be sure some people may abuse their authority and exercise power harshly (Leviticus 25:43), but that is clearly not the intention here. Humans are created in God's image, and so as his representative are expected to act in a Godlike way, and God throughout Genesis 1 and 2 is portrayed as a thoroughly creation-friendly deity. Furthermore, as I shall argue below, Genesis depicts a solidarity of humans with animals that precludes an exploitation of their power over them to their disadvantage.

But 'fill the earth and subdue it' appears to strike a different note. 'Subdue' is used elsewhere in two main senses. When people are subdued, they are often turned into slaves (Jeremiah 34:11,16; Nehemiah 5:5), which sounds harsh to modern ears though not necessarily to ancient ones (Genesis 47:19; Exodus 21:5).[6] The other sense of 'subdue' means to 'conquer' the promised land (Joshua 18:1; Numbers 32:22,29). It may be that we have here the first hint of a very important theme in Genesis, the promise of the land of Canaan. What is clear is that subduing the land is the sequel to and probably the consequence of 'multiplying and filling the earth'. Several times the Old Testament links depopulation of the land with it being overrun by wild beasts and reverting to jungle. For example 'I will not drive them [the Canaanites] out from before you in one year lest the land become desolate and the wild beasts multiply against you' (Exodus 23:29; cf. Leviticus 26:21–22; Isaiah 7:23–24; Hosea 2:12). For ancient Israelites the battle with nature was real, and without sufficient workers it would be lost. But that human beings must control their environment is not a licence for unrestrained exploitation. Genesis 1 depicts God as controlling and organising chaos, creating light, land, seas and all life, but in no way is he hostile to what he creates. It is all very good. So it follows that his appointed representatives should recognise the goodness of creation and treat it accordingly. That humans should not prey on the animals or animals attack humans is further suggested by the primeval vegetarianism of all living creatures (1:29–30).

Genesis 1 thus suggests that humans' relationship to the rest of creation should be characterised by solidarity, benevolence and control. The same positive relationship is portrayed in Genesis 2, while chapter 3 portrays its breakdown. Like humans, animals are made out of the dust of the ground, and become living beings (2:7,19). It is not said that animals have had the breath of life breathed into them as humans have, but other parallels between verses 7 and 19 imply this, as does Ecclesiastes 3:19 'they all have the same breath'. Indeed the animals are created as helpers for the humans; obviously in the pre-machine era humans were much more dependent on animals than they are today. The emphasis in this passage is of course on the fact that no animal exactly meets man's needs, which are only met by the creation of woman. But we must not overlook what is presupposed, that animals are both companions and helpers of humans. Finally the authority of humans over the animals is again asserted by Adam's naming of them: 'whatever the man called every living creature, that was its name.'(2:19)

Genesis 2 thus develops the picture of Genesis 1. It suggests that there is more to human-animal relationships than just common origin and nature. Animals are intended to be companions and helpers to humans, and to be subject to their authority. This was obviously not the case in Bible lands in Bible times and Genesis 3 shows how this state of affairs developed. The clever snake implies that it knows more than God and thus persuades the human couple to submit to its authority. This begins the eternal struggle between humans and animals focused in the danger posed by snakes:

> I will put enmity between you and the woman, and between your seed and her seed; he shall bruise your head, and you shall bruise his heel (Genesis 3:15).

Whereas traditional readers have tended to understand this text theologically as the protevangelium, the first announcement of the gospel, and liberal commentators as aetiology, why snakes bite humans, it is best to see it as both. One of the effects of the fall is hostility between humans and the animal kingdom, but ultimately the seed of Eve will triumph over the serpent's seed thus restoring humans' authority over the animals, which here also symbolise the powers of evil.[7]

More hints of the changed relationship between humans and animals are the use of animal skins to clothe Adam and Eve and the offering of animal sacrifice by Abel. Just as humans were sentenced to return to the dust as a result of the fall, so animals also experience death for the benefit of humans. However, it is the flood story that portrays most clearly the solidarity between humans and animals as well as the conflict. The flood was triggered by an earth filled with violence in which all flesh (that is humans and other living creatures) had corrupted itself. Genesis implies that it was not simply intra-human violence such as Cain and Lamech practised, it was violence between humans and animals and possibly between different animals that God objected to. This is clear after the flood when animals as well as people who take human life are sentenced to death. 'For your lifeblood I will surely require a reckoning; of every beast I will require it and of man' (9:5). Furthermore a fear of humans is imposed on the animal kingdom and permission is given to eat meat, as long as blood is not consumed (9:2–4).

But despite the intense animosity between humans and animals implied by the flood story, it does at the same time underline the solidarity between them. Noah is of course instructed not simply to save his own family but a pair of every type of animal by embarking them in the ark. The flood starts to abate when 'God remembered Noah and the beasts and all the cattle that were with him in the ark' (8:1). Much later God said to Jonah, 'Should I not pity Nineveh ... in which there more than 120,000 persons ... and also much cattle?' For his part Noah's kindness towards his animal passengers is beautifully summed up in his handling of the dove. But most striking of all is that the covenant made after the flood is not made simply between God and Noah, but 'with every living creature that is with you, the birds, the cattle, and every beast of the earth.' 'When the bow is in the clouds, I will look upon it and remember the everlasting covenant between God and every living creature' (9:10,16).

The solidarity between humans and animals is also demonstrated by the most important institution of sacrifice. It is Noah's offering of animal sacrifice that turned the anger that prompted the flood into the eternal covenant just discussed (6:5, cf. 8:21). Running through sacrificial thought is the idea of substitution, namely that in some much disputed sense the animal represents the human offerer. This is clearest in the offering of the firstborn. Originally first-born sons were consecrated to God, but by the offering of a lamb they could be redeemed (Exodus 13:2,12–13). The food laws also imply a strong connection between the human and animal worlds. Studies have shown that the realms of birds, land animals, and humans are similarly structured in biblical thought. These structures may be described over-simply as three concentric circles. The innermost circle contained birds or animals that may be sacrificed: this circle corresponds to human sacrificers, i.e. Israel's priests. The next circle consists of birds or animals which may be eaten but not sacrificed, the so-called clean animals such as sheep or goats: this circle corresponds to the chosen nation of Israel. Finally the outermost circle contains birds and animals that may never be eaten, birds of prey, carnivorous animals etc, the so-called unclean animals: these correspond to the Gentile nations. Thus in every act of worship and every meat meal the Israelite was reminded of the linkage between human and animal life and God's choice of Israel.

The dominant note in the rest of the Old Testament is of the solidarity, even intimacy, between animals and humans.[8] A good number of personal names, Deborah 'bee', Caleb 'dog', Rachel 'ewe', to mention just a few, are names of animals. In Jacob's blessing many of the tribes are compared to animals (Genesis 49). In several psalms Israel is compared to sheep. Proverbs draws various lessons from animal behaviour, while the Song of Songs likens the lovers variously to mares, doves, gazelle, a young stag, and to fawns.

But the tension between humans and animals implied in Genesis 3:15 surfaces from time to time, most notably in the plagues of Egypt when the land is successively overrun by frogs, gnats, flies, and locusts as well as other disasters. In the desert Israel was punished by fiery serpents (Exodus 8–10; Numbers 21:5–9). And the covenant curses envisage wild beasts making havoc of disobedient Israel (Leviticus 26:22). But the longterm vision is positive: once again the vision of a restored Eden with peace and harmony between humans and animals and between the different animals is held up by Isaiah. Even the carnivores will become vegetarians again in the messianic age.

> The wolf shall dwell with the lamb,
> and the leopard shall lie down with the kid,
> and the calf and the lion and the fatling together,
> and a little child shall lead them.
> The cow and the bear shall feed;
> their young shall lie down together;
> and the lion shall eat straw like the ox
> (Isaiah 11:6–7).

Debate has raged among commentators as to how literally this passage should be taken. Animals throughout the Bible are used to symbolise people and especially nations, so is Isaiah essentially just predicting peace between Israel and her enemies in this passage? Such an interpretation certainly makes good sense of what follows which predicts all nations submitting to a second David (11:10–16). It would seem to me that at least such a politico-symbolic meaning is required here, but since violence between the animals is always seen as mirroring violence between humans, a more literal understanding is also probable. It is often thought that Mark sees a fulfilment of this prophecy in Jesus' experience in the wilderness: 1:15 'he was with the wild beasts' (and was obviously not assaulted by them) indicates the dawn of the messianic age.

Thus in many ways the Old Testament vision for animals matches that of its view of plant life. Originally in God's creation there was peace and plenty, but this harmony was destroyed by sin, so that now life is a hard struggle to survive. Crops fail and animals eat each other. But in the messianic age there will be peace among people, peace between the animals, and food for all. Hosea brings all these together: 'I will make for you a covenant on that day with the beasts of the field, the birds of the air, and the creeping things of the ground; and I will abolish the bow, the sword, and war from the land ... In that day ... I will answer the heavens and they shall answer the earth; and the earth shall answer the grain, the wine, and the oil' (Hosea 2:18–21).

3. Humans' obligations to the environment

Plants

The Old Testament sees humans as God's representatives on earth, responsible for filling it with human beings and managing the other living creatures. Because they are made in God's image, humans must act in a Godlike way towards their fellow creatures. There is a solidarity between humans and animals both in nature and under the covenant, that implies a mutuality of interest: since animals are helpers to humans, Genesis implies that humans should care for animals. The Bible looks forward to a restored Eden, where water will be abundant and crops flourish, and humans and animals will live in peace together.

However reality is different. Drought, crop failure, attacks from animals and human beings characterised life from time to time in ancient as well as modern times. How does one live under these circumstances? How should humans react to aggression by plants, animals, and other human beings? How do the principles of solidarity with and benevolent rule of the environment affect daily life? How do biblical ideals and hopes modify behaviour? The laws of the Old Testament represent an uneasy compromise between ideals and the facts of daily life. For example the permission to eat meat is a concession introduced after the flood, but God still insists that blood is forbidden, because to consume it would show no respect for life. Many legislative provisions in the Pentateuch must be read this way: they define not the perfect way to live, but a floor for behaviour below which no-one dare fall without the threat of punishment.

There are few laws about plant life. Exodus 22: 5–6 insists on compensation to the owner where his crops are damaged by fire or grazing, but this is more a question of property rights than environmental protection. However, Deuteronomy's (20:19–20) ban on the cutting down of fruit trees in war to prosecute a siege does sound more environmentally motivated: 'you may eat of them, but you shall not cut them down. Are the trees in the field men that they should be besieged by you?'. When fruit trees are planted, they must be allowed to crop without being picked for three years. The fourth year's produce must be given to God, and then from the fifth year on it may be harvested normally (Leviticus 19:23–25). This patient waiting until the fifth year will ensure that they 'yield more richly for you'. It seems likely that the enhanced crop is seen as God's reward for giving to him the first fruits, not an automatic result of good horticultural practice. Throughout the law there is a requirement that first fruits of all crops, firstling domestic animals, and an annual tithe should be dedicated to God. As Proverbs 3:9–10 puts it:

> Honour the LORD with your substance
> and with the first fruits of all your produce;
> then your barns will be filled with plenty
> and your vats will be bursting with wine.

There are a number of rules on gleaning and fruit-picking designed to help the poor of society, but they do not shed any light on attitudes to plant life (Leviticus 19:9–10; Deuteronomy 23:24–25; 24:19–22). There is a strong prohibition against mixtures. 'You shall not let your cattle breed with a different kind; you shall not sow your field with two kinds of seed; nor shall there come upon you a garment of cloth made of two kinds of stuff' (Leviticus 19:19, cf. Deuteronomy 22:9–11). The motivation for the mixture ban is obscure. It may be related to the emphasis in Genesis 1 that God created all plants and living creatures 'according to their kinds'. Is it a case of 'What God has set apart, let no man confuse'? Or has it a more symbolic value related to the stern prohibition of intermarriage between Israel and the Canaanites? The food laws certainly reminded Israel of their election to be the people of God. These mixture laws could be making a similar point: Israel is different and distinct from the nations.

The law that looks most ecological in intent is that dealing with the seventh year: 'For six years you shall sow your land and gather in its yield; but the seventh year you shall let it rest and lie fallow, that the poor of your people may eat; and what they leave the wild beasts may eat' (Exodus 23:10–11, cf. Leviticus 25:2–7). Here the land is portrayed as needing a sabbath (cf. 26:34–35), though the major thrust is once again on helping the poor. Most strikingly it also helps the wild animals, who more frequently are viewed as a major threat to human survival.

This legislation while not comprehensive does seem to convey a gentle non-exploitative approach to the environment. Resting the land every seventh year, giving first fruits to God, helping the poor and even the wild beasts are the reasons appealed to in order to justify these rules. The texts suggest that maximum yields will be achieved by putting God first and letting the poor share the harvest, not by overworking the land and retaining all its fruits for oneself.

Animals

The most striking example of human solidarity with the animals comes in the Ten Commandments, the central covenantal text of the Old Testament. The Sabbath rest is for the whole household including 'your cattle' according to Exodus 20. Deuteronomy is even more specific: 'you shall not do any work ... or your ox, or your ass, or any of your cattle' (5:14). Genesis and Hosea include animals within the covenant: the Decalogue allows them to rest on the sabbath. Animals are mentioned again in the tenth Commandment against coveting.

The Ten Commandments seem to grant a moral status to animals; the laws on goring oxen appear to presuppose a degree of moral responsibility. Genesis 9:5 insists an animal which kills a human must die, but Exodus seems to underline this by insisting that the guilty ox should be killed by stoning, a method of execution usually reserved for grave offences (Exodus 21:28–32).

Striking for their humaneness are the laws dealing with the animals of an enemy. 'If you meet your enemy's ox or his ass going astray, you shall bring it back to him. If you see the ass of one who hates you lying under its burden, you shall refrain from leaving him with it, you shall help him to lift it up' (Exodus 23:4–5, cf. Deuteronomy 22:1–4). Why does the law emphasise that the animals belong to an enemy? Presumably because no-one should need encouragement to help a friend's beast. The law seems to be suggesting that even if you do not love the owner you should still love his animal.

Concern for animals' feelings seem to underline a law forbidding new-borns to be removed from their mother in the first week of life even for sacrifice, (Leviticus 22:27–29). And in any case mother and young must not be killed on the same day, a bird and its eggs or chicks must not be taken at the same time (Leviticus 22:28; Deuteronomy 22:6–7). Three times the law forbids cooking a kid in its mother's milk (Exodus 23:19; 34:26; Deuteronomy 14:21). The reasons for this ban are never explained, but it could well be a combination of outrage at the apparent heartlessness of such a custom and the subversion of the natural order that it implies: milk should be used for sustaining the kid's life not cooking it. Sustaining the life of humans, animals and plants is a recurrent element of biblical thinking and some of these laws may have a similar function: they curb practices that could jeopardise the survival of a species, e.g. killing a bird and its chicks. The ban on castrating animals (Leviticus 22:24) would seem more likely to reflect the legislator's devotion to maintaining life than concern for animal comfort. On the other hand 'You shall not muzzle an ox when it treads out the grain' is surely motivated by considerations of welfare (Deuteronomy 25:4).

As I have already said legislation sets a minimum standard of behaviour: it does not specify the ideal. An Israelite finding a bird's nest who took both mother and chicks would be breaking the law, but if he took neither he would not. Indeed he might be coming closer to the lawgiver's ideal. Proverbs 12:10 probably sums up the underlying philosophy of the Bible when it says: 'A righteous man has regard for the life of his beast, but the mercy of the wicked is cruel.' It is not simply that the righteous man wants his animal to survive, rather he cares for its *nephesh*. Though 'life' may be a suitable translation of *nephesh* sometimes, here it has more the sense of 'soul, inner self', so that we could paraphrase it 'a good man cares for the welfare of his animals'.

In examining Genesis we saw that humans and animals shared similar origins and natures and therefore there was a solidarity between them. Before the fall animals and humans lived in harmony together, but this degenerated into a universal reign of violence, which had to be regulated after the flood. The prophets look forward to a restoration of the original harmony, but in the interim the law constitutes the main means of regulating the potential violence and maintaining a semblance of order. Yet these regulations do not lose sight of the original goals of the creator. While humans' control of animals is reasserted through these laws, there is a benevolence towards other living creatures enshrined in them that expresses the solidarity between people and animals that goes back to creation. Humans, the image of God on earth, should like their creator be concerned with the living creatures they reign over: these laws show a concern not simply that animals should survive, but that those who serve humans, particularly oxen and donkeys, should be treated with kindness.

4. The Old Testament and the environment today

It is obvious that we cannot transfer Old Testament laws straight over into our modern debate. Our society is so different that a literal transfer of the rules, e.g. muzzling oxen, is out of the question. We have seen that their society depended on animals much more than we do in our mechanised age, that they felt threatened by drought, famine, and wild animals, whereas we do not. The wonderful yields obtained by modern farmers would surely have seemed like Eden to ancient Israelites. Similarly wildlife, apart from insects, bacteria and the like, has been well and truly subdued, and mankind has made great progress in filling the earth. In many respects we seem closer to the golden age looked forward to by the prophets than they were.

On the other hand if the gloomier predictions of the climatologists prove correct, we could be facing problems that will make the occasional biblical drought and famine seem trivial by comparison. The curses of Deuteronomy 28:20–24 for breaking the law will start to operate at a global scale instead of nationally. Resistant strains of bugs may wipe out crops or people despite the best efforts of modern science. How far are these threats the result of disregarding biblical principles concerning the environment?

Other questions to modern practice raised by the Bible include:

- Should we be encouraging a more vegetarian diet (cf. origins of BSE or 'mad cow disease')?

- Is genetic modification of species imitating God's creativity or is it showing disregard for the bans on mixing species?

- When does management of the earth's resources on God's behalf become exploitation by human greed? Should we make a distinction between the use of renewable and non-renewable resources?

- How far is the profit motive fostering undesirable agricultural practices? Should the biblical principles of the seventh year being fallow, dedication of first-fruits and firstlings, and tithing affect attitudes?

- How should human solidarity with animals affect attitudes towards them? Particularly in regard to conservation, veterinary practice, experimentation, pesticide use, hunting, etc? What is the proper exercise of human dominion in these spheres?

- Is the growth in human population a problem, or is it the lifestyle associated with increased wealth that is worrying?

These are some of the questions that reading the Bible in the modern world raise for me. I fear there are no easy answers. We are not living in the old Eden or the new heavens and earth. Like Israel of old we shall be forced to make compromises between our theological ideals and the situation we find ourselves in. I hope that in discussing answers to our questions that we shall not lose sight of the ethical principles and theological hopes enshrined in Scripture.

For further reading

Eaton, J. (1995) *The Circle of Creation* (London: SCM Press).
Echlin, E.P. (1999) *Earth Spirituality* (New Alresford: Arthur James).
Janowski, B. Neumann-Gorsolke, U and Glessmer, U. (1993) *Gefährten und Feinde des Menschen: Das Tier in der Lebenswelt des alten Israel* (Neukirchen-Vluyn: Neukirchener Verlag).
Linzey, A. and Yamamoto, D. (1998) *Animals on the Agenda* (London: SCM Press).
Murray, R. (1992) *The Cosmic Covenant* (London: Sheed & Ward).
Northcott, M. S. (1996) *The Environment and Christian Ethics* (Cambridge: CUP).

Notes

1. Some discussion of this theme may be found in Knierim, R.P. *The Task of Old Testament Theology*, Grand Rapids: Eerdmans, 1995, 225–243; Brueggemann, W. *Theology of the Old Testament*, Minneapolis: Augsburg, 1998, 528–551; Clines, D.J.A. *Job 1–20*, Dallas: Word, 1989, l–lii.
2. These issues are discussed in Bible dictionaries and atlases. Two full and classic treatments are Baly, D. *The Geography of the Bible*, London: Lutterworth, 1957, and de Vaux, R. *Ancient Israel*, London: Darton, Longman and Todd, 196'.
3. For a description of ancient mining see Job 28:1–11. Copper was mned at Timnah in Bible times.
4. Though the land animals are not explicitly said to be created, blessed or told to multiply, I think this is just to avoid too much repetition and give a little variety. Since everything else created on days 5 and 6 is created, blessed and multiplied, the idea carries over to the animals too.
5. For fuller discussion see Westermann, C. *Genesis 1–11*, London: SPCK. 1984, 142–155, and Wenham, G. J. *Genesis 1–15*, Waco: Word, 1987, 29–33.
6. Slavery offered security because basic needs were guaranteed by a rich employer, whereas freedom for a peasant farmer carried all the risks associated in today's society with self-employment.
7. For a fuller justification of this approach see Wenham, G. J. *Genesis 1–15*, Waco: Word, 1987, 79–81
8. On the Old Testament approach to animals, Janowski, B. Neumann-Gorsolke U. and Glessmer, U. *Gefährten und Feinde des Menschen: Das Tier in der Lebenswelt des alten Israel*, Neukirchen-Vluyn: Neukirchener Verlag, 1993, contains the most useful collection of essays on the topic.

6 – The New Testament teaching on the environment

Ernest Lucas

> The Revd Dr Ernest Lucas is Tutor in Biblical Studies, Bristol Baptist College
>
> Although the New Testament contains very little specific teaching on the environment, themes and principles, many of them pointing back to the Old Testament, can be identified.
>
> **Keywords:** New Testament, environment, Kingdom of God, redemption

Introduction

The New Testament contains very little material that can be labelled as explicitly 'teaching on the environment'. There are three good reasons for this.

1. The New Testament is not a work of systematic theology but a collection of what might be called 'occasional' writings, in the sense that each book was written for a particular audience and situation. The Gospels were written to evoke or confirm faith in Jesus as the Messiah, the Son of God and the source of salvation (while only John 20:31 states this explicitly, this seems to be true of the other Gospels too). Each gives a selective account of what Jesus said and did (cf. John 20:30), and has a particular audience in mind. Most of the Letters are written to specific church situations and deal with issues relevant to that situation. Environmental matters seem not to have been an issue on anyone's mind in the eastern Mediterranean world at the time when the New Testament writings were being written, so they do not appear explicitly in them.

2. The Old Testament forms the Scriptures of a national, political community living in its own land. Moreover, it was a community, which had a strong agricultural base to

its economy. So it is not surprising that these Scriptures contain a good deal of material about land use, treatment of animals, sharing of resources within the community, and so on, which has fairly direct relevance to modern environmental issues. The early Christian church was a multinational community, with no political power and having no identification with a particular land. Moreover, the churches to which the letters are written are all urban-based. It is therefore not surprising that the ethical issues dealt with are largely to do with personal and interpersonal matters.

3. Throughout the period during which the New Testament writings were coming into being, the Old Testament was the Scriptures of the Christian church. Hence the teaching of the Old Testament could be taken for granted. It would only need to be repeated or alluded to in areas where there was disagreement within Christian fellowships, or between Christians and Jews. Therefore, the New Testament teaching on the environment is the Old Testament teaching, in the sense that if environmental issues had become a concern to Christians in the first century, they would have turned to the Old Testament for illumination and guidance on these issues.

What all this means in practice, is that in seeking to find 'the New Testament teaching on the environment' we will often find ourselves doing one of two things. Sometimes we will be dealing with material that alludes to the Old Testament and seems to assume what it teaches. At other times we will be dealing with ideas and principles which *we* can see are relevant to environmental issues, but which are not developed in this direction in the New Testament itself.

For the sake of convenience this paper will divide up the survey of relevant material in the New Testament by looking at generally recognised sections of the New Testament. Having done that, an attempt will be made at producing a synthesis.

The Synoptic Gospels and Acts

In this section no attempt will be made to enter into the scholarly debate about how far we can get back behind the Gospels to the historical Jesus. The reason for not doing this is, first, that this is a paper about 'the teaching of the New Testament'. Secondly, in practice Christians who accept the Bible as authoritative for their faith and conduct recognise as authoritative the canonical Gospels, not a hypothetically reconstructed picture of Jesus.

At first sight there is very little in the Synoptic Gospels that is of direct relevance to our environmental concerns. Here we must not forget that Jesus accepted the Hebrew Bible as Scripture. His response to a question about divorce (Mark 10:1–9) shows that he accepted that humans were created by God, as taught in Genesis 2:4b–25. We can be sure that he would also have accepted that 'In the beginning God created the heavens and the earth' (Genesis 1:1) and what that chapter goes on to say about the nature and role of humans on the earth (Genesis 1:26–30). This belief in the createdness of the heavens and the earth and all that is in them is a mark of the apostolic preaching, especially when addressing Gentiles (Acts 14:15; 17:24–28). Jesus taught that God continues to uphold and care for his creation, both human and non-human (Matthew 6:25–30).

Mark and Matthew sum up Jesus' message as 'the time is fulfilled, and the kingdom of God/heaven has come near' (Mark 1:15; Matthew 4:17).[1] This note of 'fulfilment', that with Jesus something long-awaited has arrived, is sounded elsewhere in his teaching. Both Matthew and Luke have the saying, 'Blessed are your eyes, for they see, and your ears, for they hear. Truly I tell you, many prophets and righteous people longed to see what you see, but did not see it, and to hear what you hear, but did not hear it' (Matthew 13:16–17; Luke 10: 23–24). When John the Baptist sent some of his disciples to Jesus to enquire whether he was indeed the expected Messiah, Jesus said to them, 'Go tell John what you hear and see: the blind receive their sight, the lame walk, the lepers are cleansed, the deaf hear, the dead are raised and the poor have the good news brought to them' (Matthew 11:4–5; Luke 7:22). These words contain clear allusions to Isaiah 35:5–6; 61:1. The latter passage also occurs in Luke 4:16–30. Luke seems to use this story as the programmatic statement of Jesus' ministry instead of the shorter one found in Mark 1:15 and Matthew 4:17. Here, in the context of a synagogue service in Nazareth, Jesus reads Isaiah 61:1–2 and then says, 'Today this scripture has been fulfilled in your hearing'. Once again we are confronted with the importance of the Old Testament background, as Jesus takes up the ideas about the establishing of the rule of God in all its fullness, the Day of the Lord and the ensuing age of salvation.

Although the expression 'the kingdom of God' does not occur in the Old Testament, the idea of God as king is prominent. God is frequently spoken of as king of Israel. One way of speaking of the significance of the events at Sinai is to present it as the time when Yahweh became king of Israel: 'There arose a king in Jeshurun, when the leaders of the people assembled – the united tribes of Israel' (Deuteronomy 33:5, the context makes it clear that the 'king' is 'The LORD' mentioned in verse 2). The prophets continually remind Israel that God is their king. 'I am the LORD, your Holy One, the Creator of Israel, your King', says God through Isaiah (Isaiah 43:15). The God of Israel is also seen as the King of all the earth. Jeremiah declares, 'There is none like you, O LORD; you are great, and your name is great in might. Who would not fear you, O King of the nations?' (Jeremiah 10:6–7). The Psalms are full of references to Yahweh as universal king: 'For dominion belongs to the LORD, and he rules over the nations' (Psalm 22:28); 'Say among the nations, the LORD is king!' (Psalm 96:10). It was the Rabbi's reluctance to use the name of the God of Israel, or even the word 'God', or to use verbal expressions of God that transformed the Old Testament phrase 'the LORD reigns' into 'the kingdom of heaven'.

There is a tension in the Old Testament, because it is recognised that although God is king of all the earth *de jure*, that kingship is only partially effective *de facto* – even in Israel. The prophets therefore look forward to a time when it will be made fully effective. Isaiah says, 'On that day the LORD will punish the host of heaven in heaven, and on earth the kings of the earth ... for the LORD of hosts will reign on Mount Zion and in Jerusalem' (Isaiah 24:21,23). Zechariah looks forward to 'that day' when 'the LORD will become king over all the earth' (Zechariah 14:9). So, in the Old Testament there is a looking forward to 'the Day of the LORD' when the kingship of God over all the earth will be made fully effective. This will be a two-sided day, a day both of judgement upon evil and of salvation for the righteous. It is significant that when Jesus read from Isaiah 61 in the synagogue at Nazareth, as recorded in Luke 4:18–19, he stopped part-way through verse 2. His ministry was to inaugurate 'the year of the LORD's favour', not 'the day of vengeance of our God'. So the tension of the Old Testament remains in the New, but in a somewhat different form.

The Day of the Lord is sometimes spoken of in cosmic terms in the Old Testament. In Isaiah 34 it is the day when 'All the host of heaven shall rot away, and the skies roll up like a scroll' (v.4). However, as what follows shows, this is not the end of the cosmos, it is the end of the nation of Edom.[2] The two-sidedness of that Day is brought out in verse 8, 'For the LORD has a day of vengeance, a year of vindication by Zion's cause'. What that vindication means is described in Isaiah 35, the passage to which Jesus alluded in his reply to John the Baptist. This speaks not only of the healing of humans, but of a wider renewing of creation, with the desert blossoming 'like a crocus' (v.1–2). Taken together, Isaiah 34 and 35 seem to speak (in metaphorical terms) not of an abolition and replacement of the created order, but of a renewal and reordering of it. This seems to be true also of the 'new creation' language in Isaiah 65 and 66. The language used in Isaiah 65:17, taken on its own, might suggest abolition and replacement, 'For I am about to create new heavens and a new earth; the former things shall not be remembered or come to mind'. Again, however, what follows describes a renewed and reordered earth.[3]

This Old Testament background enables us to see that Jesus' announcement of the coming of the Kingdom of God has ecological implications, even if they are not made explicit in the Gospels. Jesus' healing miracles should not be seen in a purely human-centred perspective. They are signs of the coming renewal of the whole created order. Jesus' nature miracles have a special significance in this regard. When he stills the storm on the lake, the way he speaks and the words he uses suggest an act of exorcism.[4] It is not only humans that are under the sway of evil, needing to be set free from bondage to Satan through healing and exorcism.[5] The same is true of the non-human creation, and Jesus' work of liberation embraces both human and non-human creation. In his work as Redeemer Jesus is forwarding God's work as Creator.

Jesus expresses the core of 'kingdom ethics' in terms of the two great commandments: 'the Lord our God, the Lord is one; you shall love the Lord your God with all your heart, and with all your soul, and with all your mind, and with all your strength' and 'You shall love your neighbour as yourself' (Mark 12:29–31). Each of these commandments has implications with regard to concern for our environment. To love God must surely mean to value the creation as he values it, and to be committed to his purpose for it. Since he is working to free it from the ravages of evil, so must we. To love your neighbour as yourself is a very pro-environmental attitude. If I do not want my environment spoilt by air pollution, by-pass roads, rubbish tips, etc., then I should not wish these on my neighbours but work for them and with them to find solutions to these problems. This applies not only to neighbours in space, those who share the world with me now, but also to neighbours in time, future generations.

In the Synoptic Gospels Jesus' normal way of referring to himself is as 'the Son of Man'. There has been extensive debate about the meaning of this 'title' as used by Jesus, and about its origin.[6] However, there is considerable agreement that, as used in the Synoptic tradition, it is linked with the figure of 'one like a son of man' who appears in Daniel 7 (NB Mark 8:38; 13:26; 14:62; with parallels in the other Synoptics). In Daniel 7 this figure represents 'the holy ones of the Most High' and 'To him was given dominion and glory and kingship ... and his kingship is one that shall never be destroyed' (v.14). Clearly, this is the establishing of the universal rule of God. In the context of Daniel 7 this amounts to the completion of God's creative purpose. The vision opens with imagery borrowed from ancient near-Eastern creation stories – the raging waters and the chaos monsters. Yet the 'son of man' and 'dominion' language is reminiscent of the Hebrew understanding of creation, as found Genesis 1:26–28 and Psalm 8:3–8. It was God's intention that his 'good' creation should be ruled over and cared for by humans as his representatives. Because humans have refused to submit to God's rule, and ruled in their own name, the human powers in Daniel 7 are depicted as bestial, sub-human. Their rule is destructive. When God steps in, judges them and establishes his kingdom, it is represented by a human figure, signifying the completion of his creative purpose. Once again we see that the coming of God's kingdom does not mean the abolition of his creation, but the restoring and fulfilment of it. Such an understanding of Daniel 7 seems to be implied in Matthew 19:28, which links the coming of the Son of Man in glory with 'the renewal of all things'. There is similar language in Acts 3:21, where the return of Jesus is linked with 'the time of universal restoration'.

Given this clear understanding of the establishment of the kingdom of God as the fulfilment of creation, it is apposite that Daniel is the one book in the Old Testament with a clear understanding of the resurrection of the individual. The reaction of some of the Athenians to Paul's preaching of the resurrection ('some scoffed', Acts 17:32) points to the significance of this doctrine. In much of Greek philosophy there was a strong spirit-matter dualism. Salvation meant escaping from the material to the spiritual realm to exist as a disembodied, immaterial soul. As a result, matter was regarded as inferior, even evil. For the Hebrews, on the other hand, matter was an aspect of God's 'good' creation. It is a commonplace of Old Testament scholarship that there is no strong spirit-matter dualism in Hebrew thought. So, when individual salvation comes into focus, it is still an embodied existence that is envisaged, though in Daniel 12:3 the imagery of 'shining like stars' may imply that it is a transformed body.

All of this is relevant to understanding the full significance of the resurrection of Jesus. The Synoptic Gospels make it clear that it was a bodily resurrection. The tomb in which Jesus had been laid was empty. Luke's account emphasises the materiality of Jesus' resurrection body and its continuity with the body that was laid in the tomb. Jesus was recognisable to his friends (24:31). His body bore the scars of his crucifixion. Jesus says, 'Look at my hands and feet. Touch me and see; for a ghost does not have flesh and bones as you see I have' (24:39). Jesus then eats a piece of fish to drive the point home. Yet this is a transformed body, scars and all. It is a body that can appear and disappear at will (Luke. 24:31,36). This is the only sign we have of what the renewal and reordering of the creation might mean.

So, this survey of the Synoptic Gospels and Acts shows that, when the ministry of Jesus is understood against the background of what the Old Testament says about God's rule, the Day of the Lord and the 'one like a son of man', it becomes clear that there are implications for Christian attitudes towards our environment. They are only implications, because they are part of the understanding of God's purposes that was common ground between Jesus and his Jewish contemporaries. Those purposes involved the renewal and reordering of the whole creation, not just the saving of human beings. In this, the redemptive work of Jesus plays the vital role.

The Johannine literature

The phrase 'the kingdom of God' occurs only twice in John's Gospel (John 3:3,5). It is closely related to new birth and receiving eternal life, and it is the phrase 'eternal life' (or sometimes just 'life') that replaces it in John. Much of what is said about 'eternal life' in John parallels what is said about 'the kingdom of God/heaven' in the Synoptics. One reason for this change of terminology in John might be indicated by Acts 17:7. Some people in Thessalonica accused Paul of 'acting contrary to the decrees of the emperor, saying that there is another king named Jesus'. Clearly, while the concept of the kingdom of God was deeply meaningful to Jews, others could easily misunderstand it in purely down-to-earth political terms. Whatever the reason for this change of terminology, it seems to give John's Gospel a more 'spiritual' and less 'material' ethos in its understanding of salvation. However, this is belied by the fact that John, in both the Gospel and the letters, very clearly rejects any matter-spirit dualism.

Greeks, especially perhaps adherents of Stoicism, reading the prologue of John's Gospel would find a great deal of common ground with what is said in verses 1–13.[7] Talk of the Word, the Logos, that was divine and was active in creation and in ongoing life-giving, would be intelligible and acceptable to them. So would talk of this Logos' role in enlightening people and bringing them to God. However, for such a reader verse 14, with its bald statement that the 'the Logos became flesh', would have been shocking. This intimate uniting of the spiritual and the material was unthinkable. Yet John insists on it. It is this enfleshed Word that is the revelation of God's grace and truth to us. It is the supreme way in which God is made known to us. At the other end of his Gospel John is as clear as Luke about the material nature of Jesus' resurrection body. The tomb was empty. The body was unlike a normal body in that Jesus can appear in a locked room. Yet it is continuous with his former body because Thomas can put his finger in the nail prints and his hand in the spear wound in Jesus' side.

In the letters of John there are two key Christian 'confessions'. One is, 'Jesus is the Son of God' (1 John 4:15). The other is, 'Jesus Christ has come in the flesh' (1 John 4:2; 2 John 7). Moreover, 1 John 5:6, with its statement that Jesus Christ came 'by water and blood', is probably insisting that the one who was designated as the Son of God at his baptism by the voice from heaven died a real death on the cross. If this is so, then there is clearly an anti-Gnostic polemic here. Some Gnostics taught that the divine spirit descended on the man Jesus at his baptism but left him before he died on the cross.[8] Behind this was their strong spirit-matter dualism.

John's insistence on the materiality of Jesus' resurrection body, and so presumably ours too, might seem somewhat at odds with the only glimpse he gives us of our eternal existence. This is in John 14:2–3, 'In my Father's house are many dwelling places. If it were not so, would I have told you that I am going to prepare a place for you? And if I go and prepare a place for you, I will come again and will take you to myself'. This could be taken to imply a purely spiritual existence in heaven. In fact commentators are divided over the meaning of the 'coming again' in this passage. Some take it to refer to Jesus' coming to indwell believers through the Holy Spirit, and so unite them with the Father. Others take it as a reference to Jesus' return at the end of the age. Still others think it refers to Jesus coming to believers when they die.[9] If we do take it in an eschatological sense (whether referring to death or the end of the age), we would do best to understand it in the light of the only other picture we are given of eternal existence in the Johannine literature, in Revelation 21 and 22.

Revelation 21:1 echoes Isaiah 65:17 and, like that verse, if taken on its own could be taken to mean the total destruction of the first creation and its replacement by a new creation.

However, what follows suggests that this is not the case. John sees a new Jerusalem *coming down out of heaven*, presumably to the new earth (so our eternal existence is not in heaven). The nature of what is happening is explained in verse 5, 'See, I am making all things new'. This suggests a renewing of the old by a radical transformation, not the abolishing of it to start again *de novo*.[10,11] What follows confirms this. The kings and the peoples of the nations bring 'their glory' into it. There is continuity with the first creation, and this is a continuity to which human endeavour makes its contribution. Also, there are elements of the picture which remind us of the Garden of Eden – the river and the tree of life. God walked with Adam and Eve in that garden daily. In John's vision God and the Lamb are permanently present in the city. So, this is the culmination of the creative purpose of God as his creatures enjoy continuous fellowship with their Creator. But, we are reminded, this has been made possible by 'the Lamb that was slain' (Revelation 5:6,12), the 'Lamb of God who takes away the sin of the world' (John 1:29). It may be significant that this picture of the culmination of God's purpose is not a simple return to the Garden of Eden, but a City of Eden. In Genesis 4 the city is a human artefact, with the first one being built by Cain. This might imply that in the New Jerusalem that has come from heaven to earth God has incorporated the best of human endeavours in the working out of his purposes.

This survey shows that in the Johannine literature, as in the Synoptic Gospels, the redeeming work of Jesus cannot be separated from the achieving of God's original creative purpose. God is concerned with the renewing of the whole of creation, not with saving humans alone and discarding the rest.

The Pauline letters

For reasons similar to those given at the start of the section on 'The Synoptic Gospels and Acts' (p. 3), the letters traditionally attributed to Paul will be treated here as a whole, without entering into the debate about the apostolic authorship of some of them.

It is not surprising that Paul, a self confessed 'Hebrew of Hebrews' (Philippians 3:5), should assume the Old Testament teaching about creation. In Romans 1:20 he asserts that the created world reveals something of the nature of God, its Creator, 'Ever since the creation of the world his eternal power and divine nature, invisible though they are, have been understood and seen through the things he made'. There is an echo here of Psalm 19:1. There is also an echo of the Old Testament polemic against idolatry, which Paul characterises as worshipping and serving 'the creature rather than the Creator' (Romans 1:25).

The background of the Old Testament creation narrative is seen in Paul's comparison of Jesus to Adam. This is developed in some detail in Romans 5:12–21 and 1 Corinthians 15:20–28. Some scholars also see a Christ-Adam contrast behind the christological hymn in Philippians 2:6–11.[12] It is clear from this that for Paul Jesus marks a new beginning for the human race. This is also expressed by his use of 'new creation' language to express the state of those who are 'in Christ' (Galatians 6:15; 2 Corinthians 5:17). The same idea is expressed in Ephesians 2:15, which speaks of Christ creating 'one new humanity' which overcomes the Jew-Gentile divide.

Another way in which Paul expresses the same idea is by use of the concept of 'the image/likeness of God'. This is found only in Genesis 1:26–28; 5:1; 9:6 in the Old Testament. According to Paul, Jesus Christ is 'the image of God' (2 Corinthians 4:4; Col. 1:15). God's purpose is that humans should 'be conformed to the image of his Son' (Romans 8:29). It is in Paul's use of this 'image' concept that it becomes clear that he is not talking about God abolishing the old creation and making a new start. Rather, Paul is talking about a process of transformation of the old into the new.[13] The work of the Holy Spirit in Christians means that they are 'being transformed into the same image from one degree of glory to another' (2

Corinthians 3:18). The image of 'putting off' the old nature and 'putting on' a new one, which might seem to imply instant change and total discontinuity, is immediately qualified by saying that the new nature is 'being renewed in knowledge according to the image of its Creator' (Colossians 3:10, cf. Ephesians 4:22–24). The implication of 1 Corinthians 15:49 is that this transformation will only be completed at the resurrection of the body.

Where will people spend eternity in transformed, resurrection bodies? There is no clear answer to this in the Pauline literature. However, it is worth pointing out a fairly common misreading of 1 Thessalonians 4:16c, 17. Paul says that when Christ returns 'the dead in Christ will rise first; then we who are alive, who are left, shall be caught up together with them in the clouds to meet the Lord in the air; and so we shall always be with the Lord'. It is sometimes assumed that the place where we shall 'always be with the Lord' is elsewhere, and so we go to meet him in the air, part-way on the journey to heaven. This, in fact, totally misses the point of the imagery Paul is using here. In verse 15 Paul uses the word *parousia* to speak of this 'coming' of the Lord at the end of the age. This is the word used of the visit of a ruler, or some other very important person, and his entourage to a city, when he would be met outside the city by a deputation from it, which would escort him into the city.[14] Paul, therefore, is thinking of believers going to 'meet the Lord in the air' in order to escort him to the earth – so is that where 'we shall always be with the Lord'?

Whatever we conclude about the implications of 1 Thessalonians 4:16c–17, it is clear that, as far as humans are concerned, the redemptive work of Christ is seen by Paul as the consummation of God's purpose for humans when he originally created them in God's image and likeness. But is Paul interested in a broader redemption of creation? Two aspects of his thought show that he is. The first finds expression in Romans 8:18–25. There has been much debate over the details of this passage. We can only pick up on a few points.[15] Some commentators have argued that *ktisis* here should be taken in the sense 'the creature' and as referring to human beings. However, both the general context and specifically verse 20a (with the phrase 'not of its own will') lead most to understand it in the sense 'the creation', meaning the sub-human creation. It seems best to take *mataiotes* (futility) in its natural sense of 'something that does not function as it was designed to and so does not attain its goal'. The word *phthora* is used by Greek writers of dissolution and decay in the world of nature. The general picture conveyed here by Paul is that human disobedience of God means that the natural order cannot achieve its goal, indeed is falling into disorder.[16] Yet there is hope. The redemption of humans by Christ is the central part of a wider redemptive work, involving the whole created order. What it will mean for the rest of creation to 'obtain the freedom of the children of God' (v.21b) is not explained. However, the linking of this hope with 'redemption of our bodies' (v.23b) gives us a clue to what might be in Paul's mind. It points us to 1 Corinthians 15:35–49 with its imagery of the seed and the plant that grows from it. This combines both continuity and transformation. The old creation is not simply abolished, but is transformed. This, of course, parallels what we have already seen to be true of the way Paul presents the transformation into a 'new creation' that goes on in the individual who is 'in Christ'. Both the renewing work of the Holy Spirit in the believer, and the resurrection of the body provide the same kind of 'model' for understanding the ultimate renewal of the whole of creation. The other aspect of Paul's thought which shows that his perspective regarding Christ's work is wider than just the salvation of humans is the cosmic significance that is given to Christ in Colossians 1:15–20. In this passage the outcome of Christ's work is cosmic reconciliation and restoration to harmony. This passage brings together creation and redemption because Christ the

Redeemer is the same Christ who is the Creator and the Sustainer of the created order.

Paul sees a linkage between the work of Christ in reconciling humans to God and to each other and a reconciling of 'all things' to God. Moreover, Christians have been given a 'ministry of reconciliation' which flows from Christ's work (2 Corinthians 5:18–20). Does this have any relevance with regard to ecological issues? Given that Paul insists that Christians should use their redeemed physical bodies (even though that redemption will only be complete at the resurrection of the body) in ways that glorify God (1 Corinthians 6:19–20; Romans 12:1), there is at least the implication that the same should be true of our use of the redeemed sub-human creation (even thought its full redemption awaits ours).

Peter's letters

Some Christians appeal to 2 Peter 3:7–13 as a reason for not getting involved in environmental issues. This passage, they say, speaks of the utter destruction of the present cosmos by fire and its replacement by a new one. The implication seems to be that this physical order has no ultimate place in God's purposes, so why should Christians bother about issues of conservation and ecology? A glance at this passage in a few modern English translations will show that there are problems of translation, especially in verse 10. Consultation of the more detailed commentaries will show that this is indeed a passage that is difficult to understand.[17] Here we can only touch on a few of the major issues, and indicate what seems to be a growing consensus on its meaning.

Probably *the* key issue is a textual one, concerning the final word of verse 10. There is a wide variety of readings in the surviving manuscripts, the main options being: 'will be found', 'will disappear', 'will be burned up'. There is little doubt among textual scholars that the earliest and best reading is 'will be found'. Despite this, many English translations have adopted the reading 'will be burned up', presumably because it makes the most obvious sense. However, together with its later and more limited attestation in the manuscripts, this is the very reason for suspecting that it is not the original reading, but was introduced as a change to ease the sense.

A second issue is the meaning of the word *stoicheia* in this passage. The translation 'elements' leads many modern readers to presume that the reference is to the elements of which all physical things are composed. This is a possible meaning. In the Pauline letters the word is used to refer to the (hostile) spiritual powers which rule over the created order (Galatians 4:3; Colossians 2:8,20). Some see support for this meaning here too because Peter seems to be echoing Isaiah 34:4, with its reference to the 'the host of heaven', meaning the spiritual powers. Many take the word as referring to the heavenly bodies, the sun, moon and stars. This is a well-attested sense of the word in the second century AD. Since in both Jewish and pagan circles the heavenly bodies were often thought of as controlled by spiritual beings, the latter two meanings would probably be closely allied in the mind of the writer of 2 Peter. Because throughout this passage there is a heaven-earth pairing, and because in both of its occurrences it is preceded by a reference to 'the heavens', it seems more likely that *stoicheia* refers to 'heavenly beings' of some kind than to the physical elements.

So what does this passage mean? First of all, the clear echoes of Isaiah 34 are significant. They point to the fact that the writer is heir to a long tradition of *figurative* language about 'cosmic events'. We have seen that this can be applied to 'normal' events within history which are seen as acts of God's judgement. Hence we should be wary of reading it as a literal account of the end of the physical cosmos. The second thing we need to recognise is that the theme is God's final act of judgement (v.7), not cosmological speculation about the end of the physical universe. Once the judgement theme is seen as primary, a good deal falls into place. Sense can be made of the reading 'will be found' at the end of verse 10. The verb 'to find' is used in the Old Testament in judicial and quasi-judicial contexts of moral and judicial scrutiny, e.g. Exodus 22:8; Psalm 17:3; Daniel 5:27. In the Bible the passive form of a verb sometimes conceals a reference to God as agent. So, the end of verse 10 refers to the judgement of the earth and all the deeds done on it by God. But to what does the earlier part of the verse refer? In the Old Testament (e.g. Isaiah 24:21; 34:5) judgement of the heavenly powers precedes, or accompanies, judgement on earth. That may be all that is in mind in 2 Peter 3, though the use of the phrases 'dissolved with fire' (v.10) and 'melt with fire' (v.12) may suggest destruction of the physical 'heavenly bodies' as well. However, in the Old Testament fire is used as a metaphor of judgement which does not simply destroy, but *purifies*, e.g. Isaiah 21–26; Malachi 1–4. The language of 'dissolving/melting' would fit in with the figurative use of the idea of fire refining impure metals.

All this points to the primary reference of verses 7–12 being to the ultimate act of God's judgement, which will purge the created order of all evil. The language used is drawn from a long tradition in which this kind of language is used figuratively of acts of God within history. How far the writer would have regarded it as literal in this case we cannot really be sure. What is clear is that the main point is that out of this act of judgement come a new heaven and a new earth (v.13). If taken strictly, the parallel with the Flood (v.5–6) suggests that while the event may be a cataclysmic one, there is still considerable continuity between the worlds before and after purifying judgement.[18] There may well be an implication of continuity in the Greek word used for 'new' (*kainos*) in verse 13. Although the earlier clear distinction between *kainos* (new in quality) and *neos* (previously non-existent) was blurred by New Testament times, that distinction seems to be there in most of the occurrences of these words in the New Testament.[19] So, although 2 Peter 3 is speaking of a radical transformation of the heaven and the earth, it is a renewal through transformation, not a total destruction of the old and its replacement by something quite different.[20] It does not in fact stand in opposition to this theme, which we have seen runs through the Synoptic, Johannine and Pauline strands of the New Testament. It is certainly not a basis for arguing against Christian concern for, and involvement in, ecological issues.

The Letter to the Hebrews

The author of this letter alludes to Genesis 1 and the creation of the world by the word of God in chapter 11:3. However, in the opening verse of the letter he gives the act of creation a christological slant by speaking of the Son as the one through whom God created the world and who is 'heir of all things' (1:2). Moreover, the Son 'sustains all things by his powerful word' (1:3). Here the Son is given the same cosmic significance as in Colossians 1:15–20. Once again creation and redemption are inter-connected, because the Son is also the one who has 'made purification for sins' (1:3). In Hebrews 1:1–4 the Son is presented as sharing the deity of the God of Israel. Yet in Hebrews 2 this same Son is spoken of as becoming a true human being (2:14,17). This is a genuine incarnation of God.

The way the writer approaches the subject of the incarnation is significant. He begins by quoting Psalm 8:4–6, which itself echoes Genesis 1:26–28. We are told that the incarnation happened to bring to completion the as yet unrealised purpose of God in creating human beings, that they should rule creation as God's representatives. There is a close parallel here to what we saw to be the significance of the use of 'Son of Man' as a title for Jesus in the Synoptic Gospels. What was implied in Hebrews 1:3 is made clear in chapter 2:5–9. The work of redemption is also the completion of God's purpose for his creation. It is, perhaps, because the Son becomes the perfect human being who is 'crowned with glory and honour' (i.e. is the image of God as humans should be) that he is 'heir of all things'. The created order becomes his inheritance as the Son who has brought 'many children to glory' (2:10, i.e. to the true realisation of their humanness). For Christians there is a strong motivation here for caring for the creation. Genesis 1:26–28 presents humans as God's vice-regents or stewards caring for his creation and answerable to him for their use of it. The implication of Hebrews 1:2 and 2:5–10 is that Christians are the trustees of the inheritance of their 'elder brother' and Saviour until he comes to claim it.

Synthesis

Our survey of the New Testament has uncovered some key themes which run through all or most of the sections we have looked at.

1. The New Testament does not allow any separation between God's purpose in creation and in redemption. We have followed a number of themes which are often thought of primarily as ways of understanding God's work of redemption through Christ: the in-breaking of the kingdom of God, the Day of the Lord as the day of salvation and of judgement, Jesus as the Son of Man, the purpose of the incarnation. Each has been found to be wider in scope than simply the salvation of human beings from sin and death. Each has led us to see that the redemptive work of Christ is related to the fulfilment of God's purpose for the whole of the created order, not just humans. At the very least this means that those who work for the preservation and enhancement of the goodness of God's creation are working with the grain of God's purposes. But it is legitimate to go beyond that and see the 'ministry of reconciliation' to which Christians are called to be wider in scope than it usually has been. Of course at the heart of it is the reconciling of women and men to God. It is generally recognised that this then implies the work of reconciling people to one another, Jew to Gentile, oppressor to oppressed, myself to my enemy. 'Blessed are the peacemakers, for they shall be called children of God' said Jesus (Matthew 5:9). Surely the work of reconciliation should also involve reconciling humans to the non-human creation, by working to bring people to exercise the dominion we do have over creation in the way we are intended to exercise it. This is a way that reflects the nature of God – with wisdom, justice and love. The last few decades have seen a new emphasis on the church's healing ministry. This has been understood in the narrow sense of bringing healing of various kinds to humans. A wider view of the church's 'ministry of reconciliation' would extend this to the healing of the 'wounds' which humans have inflicted on the non-human creation.

2. The destiny of the non-human created order depicted in the New Testament is not that of a throw-away container which God will discard when Christ finally comes to consummate the salvation of humans. Rather, the final salvation of humans is part of a wider renewal of the whole creation through transformation. As John Polkinghorne has put it, the new creation will not be the result of the annihilation of the present one and then another act of *creatio ex nihilo*, but will be the result of an act of *creatio ex vetere*.[21] The only 'models' we have of this 'renewal through transformation' are those of the recreating work of the Holy Spirit in the believer and the resurrection body of Christ. In both there is an element of discontinuity (more obvious in the second 'model') and of continuity (more obvious in the first 'model'). In various places in the New Testament there are hints that what humans do now can make a contribution to the new creation (e.g. Revelation 21:24, 26; 1 Corinthians 3:14; 2 Corinthians 4:16–18). Our ecological labours will not be in vain if done in the Lord (1 Corinthians 15:58).

3. The incarnation of the Word who 'was with God and was God' (as John puts it), who was also the Son 'who is the outflow of the glory of God and bears the very stamp of his nature' (as Hebrews put it) shows that Christianity should have no place for a strong spirit-matter dualism that denigrates the material world. God can be made known in and through it. Moreover, the doctrine of the resurrection of the body says that God will take up the material and transform it, not discard it. Our eternal destiny is not a disembodied existence in a purely spiritual heaven, but an embodied existence on a transformed earth.

These key themes provide a solid biblical and theological basis for Christian concern about, and involvement in, environmental issues.

This theological basis ought to act as a motivation for Christians to get involved in care for the environment. Our survey has raised some more specific motivations within this more general one.

1. There is the **ethical** motivation provided by the two great commandments enunciated by Jesus. We said above that to love God implies caring for the things for which he cares, and being committed to the same purposes as he is. As our survey shows, God does care about the non-human creation. Jesus' words about God's care of the birds and flowers (Matthew 6:26–30) underscores this. For this reason God will not simply discard it but take it up, in a transformed state, into the new heaven and the new earth. We also noted the profound relevance of the command to 'love your neighbour as yourself' for environmental matters. The 'golden rule', 'whatever you wish that others would do to you, do so to them' (Matthew 7:12) expresses one way in which this command can be made more specific.

2. There is an **evangelistic** motivation, which arises from the point Paul makes in Romans 1:20 that the creation reveals something of the nature of the Creator. It is a fact that, for some people at least, 'communing with nature' leads to a heightening of spiritual awareness and a seeking after the Creator. The despoiling of nature leads to a loss of this 'evangelistic' opportunity for the creation to 'tell the gory of God' and to 'proclaim his handiwork' (Psalm 19:1). Here is one reason for the preservation of areas of 'natural' beauty such as National Parks for the general public to enjoy. It also applies to Sites of Special Scientific Interest where the specialist can 'think God's thoughts after him'.

3. There is an **eschatological** motivation in the concept that we are trustees of the inheritance which Christ will one day come to claim. We rooted this concept in Hebrews 1:2, but it is also implied in Colossians 1:16, which says of Christ that 'all things were created through him and *for him*'.

So, we have seen that the New Testament provides us with a theological basis for concern about the environment, and some specific motivations for getting involved in the environmental issues of our day. It does not provide us with detailed principles on which to base environmental policies or give us specific guidance for particular situations. The reasons for this were explained in the introduction above. Therefore we find ourselves having to do what the first Christians did not need to do, turn to the Old Testament to see what more detailed guidance we can derive from its teaching.

Notes

1. For a good survey of the material about the kingdom of God/heaven in the Gospels, with a bibliography, see the article by C.C. Caragounis on 'Kingdom of God/Kingdom of Heaven' in Green, J.B., McKnight, S. and Marshall I.H. (eds), *Dictionary of Jesus and the Gospels*, Leicester: IVP, 1992, 417–430.
2. Kaiser, O., in *Isaiah 13–39*, London: SCM, 1974, 357, comments that since in chapter 35 the prophet 'clearly assumes that the geographical circumstances of the earth will continue to exist' the picture painted in 34:4 is used 'only as an image for the cosmic terrors associated with the day of Yahweh'.
3. Westermann, C., in *Isaiah 40–66*, London: SCM, 1969, 408, says, 'The words "I create anew the heavens and the earth" do not imply that the heaven and earth are to be destroyed and in their place a new heaven and earth created ... Instead, the world, designated as "heaven and earth" is to be miraculously renewed'. Watts, J.D.W., in *Isaiah 34–66*, Waco, Texas: Word Books, 1987, 354, gives a more historical interpretation. He takes the 'new heavens and new earth' language to represent 'the new order, divinely instituted, which chaps. 40–66 have revealed and in which the Persian Empire has Yahweh's sanction and Israel is called to be a worshipping and a pilgrim people with Jerusalem as its focus'.
4. Anderson, H., in *The Gospel of Mark*, London: Oliphants, 1976, 145, says, ' "Peace! Be still!" are in the Greek "Silence! Be muzzled!" and the latter (cf. Mk. 1:25) features in wonder- worker stories almost as a technical term for dispossessing a demon of his power'.
5. There is not space here to discuss the issue of how the 'Fall' is best understood. Christians have tended to polarise around 'ontological' and 'relational' understandings of it. The former hold that there was a change in the physical being of things. The latter see the results of the Fall in terms of changes in relationships. In my view the relational view accords better both with the nature of the story in Genesis 3 and with the reality of the evidence for the natural

history of the earth. The act of disobedience broke the proper relationship between humans and God. The result was a breakdown of other key relationships. Individuals are no longer at peace with themselves (Adam and Eve felt shame), or with one another (Adam blamed Eve). The harmonious relationship between humans and the rest of creation has been disturbed (the cursing of the ground). But this has given evil an entrance into the world which it would otherwise not have. This is the truth represented by the Pauline reference to the 'principalities and powers' and their influence over the world and humans.

6. On this debate see the article by I.H. Marshall on 'Son of Man' in Green, J.B., McKnight, S. and Marshall I.H. (eds) *Dictionary of Jesus and the Gospels*, Leicester: IVP, 1992, 775–781.
7. Odd, C.H. *The Interpretation of the Fourth Gospel*, Cambridge: CUP, 1953, 263–285.
8. Marshall, I.H. *The Epistles of John*, Grand Rapids: Eerdmans, 1978, 231–233.
9. The verb 'come' in verse 3 is present tense in the Greek, perhaps emphasising a continuing event (which would favour the idea of Jesus' coming to indwell the believer, as might verse 23). However, the verb 'take' is future tense in the Greek, allowing the possibility that 'come' should also be read as future (and so allowing the reference to be to either the death of the believer or the coming of Jesus at the end of the age). See the brief discussion in Barrett, C.K. *The Gospel According to John*, SPCK, 1956, 381–382.
10. Beasley-Murray, G.R., in *The Book of Revelation*, London: Oliphants, 1974, 312 comments on Revelation 21:5, 'The word order should be observed, "Behold, new am I making all things!" The emphasis is on the newness which God imparts to his creation, and therefore to his creatures. He is not discarding them, but granting them to know the newness of life manifest in the risen Christ, and operative even in this age in all who are in Christ'.
11. Bauckham, R., in *The Theology of the Book of Revelation*, Cambridge, CUP, 1993, 49, says, 'the contrast between "the first heaven and the first earth" on the one hand, and "the new heaven and the new earth" on the other, refers to the eschatological renewal of this creation, not its replacement by another'.
12. Hawthorne, G.F., in *Philippians*, Waco, Texas: Word Books, 1983, 82–33, discusses this interpretation briefly.
13. See the article by Clines D.J.A. on 'Image of God' in Hawthorne, G.F., Martin, R.P. and Reid D.G. (eds) *Dictionary of Paul and His Letters*, Leicester: IVP, 1993, 426–428.
14. On this see Kittel G. and Friedrich G. (eds), *Theological Dictionary of the New Testament, Vol. 5*, 859–860 and Bruce, F.F. *1&2 Thessalonians*, Waco, Texas: Word Books, 1982, 57.
15. Cranfield, C.E.B., in *The Epistle to the Romans, Vol. 1*, Edinburgh: T. & T. Clark, 1975, 404–420, provides a very full discussion of this passage.
16. Dunn, J.D.G., in *The Theology of the Apostle Paul*, Edinburgh: T&T Clark, 1998, 100, says 'Creation has been caught up in the futility of human self-deception. For humankind to think that it stands in relation to the rest of creation as creator to creation ("You shall be like God") imposes futility as much on creation as on humankind itself. There is an out-of-joint-ness about creation which its human creatures share (8.22–23). But as creation shares in humankind's futility, so it will share in humankind's liberation from "the slavery of corruption" (8.21)'.
17. Bauckham, R.J. in *Jude, 2 Peter*, Waco, Texas: Word Books, 1983, 298–335, provides a detailed discussion of the textual problem and the issues of interpretation in these verses.
18. Bauckham, *op. cit.* ref. 9, 49f, makes this point.
19. Brown, C. (ed.) *The New International Dictionary of New Testament Theology, Vol. 2*, 669f, article on 'New' says, 'In the course of time the differences of meaning between *neos* and *kainos* became blurred, even to the point of occasional synonymity. But the NT has significantly used *kainos* with its more

qualitative sense in order to give expression to the fundamentally new character of the advent of Christ'.
20. Bauckham, *op. cit.* ref. 13, 326, says of 2 Peter 3:10,12, 'Such passages emphasize the radical discontinuity between the old and the new, but it is nevertheless clear that they intend to describe a renewal not an abolition of creation'.
21. Polkinghorne, J., in *Science and Christian Belief*, London: SPCK, 1994, 167, says 'the new creation is not a second attempt by God at what he had first tried to do in the old Creation. It is a different kind of divine action altogether, and the difference may be summarized by saying that the first creation was *ex nihilo* while the new creation will be *ex vetere*. In other words, the old creation is God's bringing into being a universe which is free to exist "on its own", in the ontological space made available by the divine kenotic act of allowing the existence of something wholly other; the new creation is the divine redemption of the old'.

7 – The New Testament teaching on the environment: A response to Ernest Lucas

Richard Bauckham

> Richard Bauckham is Professor of New Testament Studies and Dean of the Faculty of Divinity, University of St Andrews, Scotland
>
> There is a distinction between the urban and the rural in New Testament times and now. A key theme is our place is beside our fellow creatures as fellow worshippers, a necessary counterbalance to the hierarchical idea of human dominance over creation.
>
> **Keywords:** New Testament, environment, Worship

There is little from which I dissent in Ernest Lucas's excellent survey and synthesis. I think there is much to discuss about the implications of Lucas's material when contextualized in our contemporary context – a stage of discussion which his paper barely broaches – but I think (and I think he would agree) that such discussions need to be based on the teaching of the two testaments of the Bible together, not on the NT alone. In my limited space, I will confine myself to some (I think important) refinements and additions to his work.

The urban and the rural then and now

Lucas remarks that 'the churches to which the letters are written are all urban-based', and that it is 'therefore not surprising that the ethical issues dealt with are largely to do with personal and interpersonal matters' (Introduction). Both statements are true, but I am doubtful about the alleged connection between them, which seems to me based on the unconscious use of a modern understanding of 'urban.' Most ancient 'cities' were by modern standards very small, and their close relationship with and dependence on the surrounding countryside was obvious and a matter of ordinary conscious awareness. Urban people were not alienated from the natural world in the way that has become normal for modern city-dwellers, surrounded by a human-made environment and human-made objects whose derivation from nature is too remote to make the connection conscious. A nice biblical illustration is Mark 15:21: Simon of Cyrene is on his way back to his home in Jerusalem after a morning spent working on, presumably, the plot of land he owned or rented somewhere outside the city. Upper class people lived in cities but usually owned large estates elsewhere. People who made money in other ways (i.e. trade) put it into agriculture and aspired to become landed aristocracy. Paul's letters to his urban Christian communities frequently use agricultural illustrations (Romans 11:16–24; 1 Corinthians 3:5–9; 15:36–37; Galatians 6:7–9), as does James (James 3:12; 5:7). Moreover, while the letters are (perhaps not all, but mostly) addressed to urban communities, the Gospels depict a largely rural audience for Jesus' teaching, which is rich in reference to aspects of nature and agricultural life. Thus, to understand the vast difference between our world and the Bible's, in terms of people's lived relationship with the non-human creation, we must really take on board the fact that the Bible's world is pre-industrial and that this made both living in towns and living on the land very different from both urban (increasingly post-industrial) and rural life today. Ancient literature of all kinds simply takes for granted that human life is embedded in the rest of nature and inextricable from it. But modern biblical interpretation (up to recent attempts to base an ecotheology biblically) has persistently ignored what the texts assume and say about the human relationship to nature, assuming, as modern urban and technological people do, that references to nature can only be picturesque illustrations of human life, and reading the modern ideology of human emancipation from nature into the texts. This modern ideology powerfully influenced modern biblical theology with its strong tendency to set history against nature and salvation against creation (thus forming a kind of modern equivalent to Platonism in its attempt to detach humans from nature). To read the texts ecologically we have to make the effort to think in a creation- embedded way which will catch the resonances of texts for which constant and immediate relationship with non-human nature is as everyday and unremarkable as relationship with the built environment is for modern urban people.

No environmental concern?

'Environmental issues do not seem to have been on anyone's mind' in the first century (Introduction). It is probably true that people were not aware of the serious deforestation and desertification which some ancient farming was already causing, or of the extinction of species by human action, which was rare (the Syrian elephant, a third elephant species, was close to extinction by the first century, and the Roman aristocracy's taste for using ivory on a huge scale was wiping out the African elephant population in its more northern areas, requiring the increasing import of Indian ivory instead), though historians of antiquity and classical scholars have until recently been so little interested in such matters that it would be rash to say there is no evidence of environmental concern of these types to be found. But the important point to make is that, while ancient people did not share our environmental concerns, i.e. they did not recognize themselves as a threat to nature, they were often very aware of nature as a threat to themselves. In other words, the dominant problematic aspect of the human relation to the rest of nature was for them the reverse of what it is for us. Earthquakes, shipwrecks, drought and famine, locust plagues, dangerous wild animals, animals that steal livestock or crops, extreme cold and extreme heat, undrinkable water, and so on – we need to realise how nature in such guises impacted peasants close to poverty (most ancient people) or travellers (many first century people for one reason or another) or even urban people whose food came straight from the land around the town. Nature often seemed hostile. Whereas for us the healing of the relationship between humans and the rest of creation most obviously suggests that humans stop destroying nature, for them it most obviously suggested that nature be friendlier to humans (so, e.g. Isaiah 11:6–9). For us to identify and understand biblical texts which treat the relationship of humans and nature, it is important we recognize this sense in which they usually approach it from a different angle from ours. This makes Jesus' stilling of the storm intelligible. Lucas correctly (unlike most biblical scholars who cannot believe the human relationship to nature was of any serious interest to the evangelists or their readers) recognizes the ecological theme of this story, but it is the greater once we recognize that the story is told in such a way as to evoke the mythic dimension of the sea as the forces of chaos, the vast resources of destructive power in nature. By commanding the sea, Jesus acts as God (who alone can order the winds and the waves), recalling God's action in creation and anticipating the new creation (in which there will be no sea, as Revelation 21:1, using a different image, has it). (For our context it is important to notice that Jesus' action is depicted as uniquely divine; there is no warrant here for human technological domination of nature.) It also becomes very interesting that in Romans 8, Paul rather unusually sees the problem God must deal with, not as nature's hostility to us, but as nature's suffering because of us (in whatever sense he means that). But there is a kind of parallel (perhaps source) in the story of the flood (Genesis 6:11–13) which finds its eschatological echo in Revelation 11:18 (God will 'destroy the destroyers of the earth').

A key theme omitted: the worship of God by the non-human creation

Lucas correctly argues that the NT for the most part presumes the OT teaching about creation, without needing to repeat it. This point bears emphasis against the still influential tendency of many Christians to think of the OT as out-dated by the NT. I have argued elsewhere[1] that references to animals in Jesus' teaching are much more significant than usually recognized because they amount to a firm endorsement of the attitudes to animals found in the OT and Jewish tradition. But there is one extremely significant (for us in our context) theme in the OT's discourse about the non-human creation that Lucas does not mention as recurring importantly in the NT: the worship of God by the non-human creation, portrayed in the Psalms (e.g. Psalm 148) and, with christological and eschatological character, in the NT (Philippians 2:10; Revelation 5:13). All creatures, animate and inanimate, worship God. This is not, as modern biblical interpreters so readily suppose, merely a poetic fancy or some kind of primitive animism. The creation worships God just by being itself, as God made it, existing for God's glory. (There is no indication in the Bible of the notion that the other creatures need us to voice their praise for them. This idea, that we are called to act as priests to nature, mediating, as it were, between nature and God, is quite often found in recent Christian writing, but it intrudes our inveterate sense of superiority exactly where the Bible will not allow it.) The key point implicit in these depictions of the worship of creation is the intrinsic value of all creatures, in the theocentric sense of the value given them by their Creator and offered back to him in praise. In this context, our place is beside our fellow-creatures as fellow-worshippers. In the praise in which we gratefully confess ourselves creatures of God there is no place for hierarchy. Creatureliness levels us all before the otherness of the Creator. This biblical theme is a necessary counterbalance to the hierarchical relationship portrayed in the Genesis idea of dominion over creation. It is a vital biblical resource to prevent the abuse and over-use of that dominion.

I am strongly inclined to connect the four living creatures (Revelation 4–5) with this theme. If creation needs priests, here they are in heaven, the central worshippers in creation, worshipping continuously in the immediate presence of God and doing so representatively, offering all creation's worship until the time when all creation will perfectly and fully follow them in their worship (Revelation 5:13; only then do the living creatures say 'Amen': v.14). If this is the role of the living creatures, then it is noteworthy that of these 'heavenly animals' (this is how Ezekiel and Revelation seem to depict them, as distinct from angels, who are depicted as heavenly humans') only one has a human face. That one is our representative, but the others represent the wild mammals (lion), domestic animals (ox) and birds (eagle). (These are the three most obvious categories of non-human animals, for ancient people, and I take it that, since this is all symbolism, they are not meant exclusively of other categories of animals.)

Imitating God's compassion for all his creatures

Lucas sees a duty to care for what God cares for implicit in the command to love God. But there is a more direct route to this end, if we read the NT not in isolation, as it was never meant to be read, but canonically and inter-textually with the OT, thus:

> Luke 6:36: 'Be merciful [*oiktirmones*, a word almost always used of God], just as your Father is merciful [*oiktirmon*].'
> Psalm 145:8–9: 'YHWH is gracious and merciful, slow to anger and abounding in steadfast love.
> [This is the classic biblical revelation of the character of God: Exod 34:6.]
> YHWH is good to all, and his compassion [LXX: *hoi oiktirmoi autou*] is over all that he has made.'

Jesus' messianic peace with wild animals (Mark 1:13)

In addition to the Gospel material which Lucas highlights as relevant to an ecological reading of the Gospels as concerned with the human relationship with non-human nature, I have discussed at length elsewhere[2] the ecological significance of Mark's reference to the fact that Jesus in the wilderness was 'with the wild animals'. Briefly, Jesus in the wilderness, following his baptism and appointment as Messiah, is establishing his messianic relationship with the non-human world (Satan, the wild animals, angels) before going on to fulfil his messianic commission in the human world. Of the three non-human categories, Satan is hostile, the angels friendly, but between them the animals – as we know from OT and Jewish tradition – equivocal, usually experienced as threats to humans, but in God's purpose destined for peaceable relations with humanity in the messianic age (Isaiah 11:6–9). Jesus makes friends of these potential enemies. The very simple 'was with the wild animals' suggests a friendly being-with – not human domination over, not making them servants (as some postbiblical Jewish eschatology expected), but letting them be themselves, leaving them their wilderness, peaceably affirming them as creatures who share the world with us in the community of God's creation. In his messianic person, he establishes representatively the restoration of the paradisal state that the OT expects in the messianic age. It may be useful sometimes, instead of the very abstract or generalized language in which theology and biblical interpretation tend to speak of the eschatological future of the non-human creation, if they speak of it at all, to think of the species Jesus would have encountered in the Judean wilderness (some of them now extinct in Palestine by human fault) – hyenas, jackals, desert foxes, hares, porcupines, antelopes, wild asses, ostriches, bears, and many others. These specific creatures of God, like all others, have a future in God's new creation.

Notes

1. Chapter 4 (Jesus and Animals I: What did he Teach?) and chapter 5 (Jesus and Animals II: What did he Practise?) in Linzey A. and Yamamoto D. (eds) *Animals on the Agenda: Questions about Animals for Theology and Ethics*, London SCM Press, 1998, 33–60.
2. 'Jesus and the wild animals (Mark 1:13): a Christological image for an ecological age', in Green J.B. and Turner M. (eds) *Jesus of Nazareth: Lord and Christ. Essays on the Historical Jesus and New Testament Christology*, FS for I. Howard Marshall, Grand Rapids: Eerdmans, 1994, 3–21; cf. also Linzey A. and Yamamoto D. (eds) *Animals on the Agenda: Questions about Animals for Theology and Ethics*, London: SCM Press, 1998, 54–60.

8 – Christians, environment and society
Michael S. Northcott

> The Revd Dr Michael S. Northcott is in the Faculty of Divinity, New College, University of Edinburgh
>
> The natural sciences have a less significant role than the social sciences in both explaining the reasons for environmental damage and for constructing mechanisms for its amelioration.
>
> **Keywords:** climate change, politics, the poor, economics, rights

Introduction

One of the constitutive aims of The John Ray Initiative is to demonstrate 'how the natural and social sciences and technology can be harnessed to protect the environment and ameliorate environmental damage'. In this paper I examine briefly the contribution of the natural and social sciences to the major environmental problem of global warming and climate change. I propose that the natural sciences have a less significant role than the social sciences in explaining the causes of global warming and in constructing mechanisms for its amelioration. I also note that while it is the rich nations in the temperate zones, in particular in the North, which are generating the majority of excess greenhouse gases, it is the poorer nations in the tropical zones in the South which are carrying most of the costs of climate change. I propose that the problem of climate change is interconnected with the distribution of wealth and resources in the global economy and that a possible mechanism for righting such global environmental wrongs is the extension of the legal recognition of human rights to include the right to a healthy environment in both national and international law and treaty. I propose that this legal recognition expresses the principle of natural right to the means of sustenance as we encounter it in the economic laws of ancient Israelite society as recorded in the Hebrew Bible. I also propose that the recognition of environmental rights gives expression to the Christian principle of love, and not just of legalistic justice, for it has the potential to enhance the rights of poor people in relation to the presently much more powerful rights of corporations and wealthy nation states, reflecting the divine intention as expressed in the incarnation to 'lift up the (environmentally) poor'.

Science, society and environment

There is a widespread assumption amongst scientists and civil servants that science has 'the answers' to environmental problems: first in firming up predictions about global environmental change through published scientific research, sometimes co-ordinated through international organs such as the Intergovernmental Panel on Climate Change (IPCC), and second in identifying scientific fixes and alternative technologies which reduce the environmental impacts of human production and consumption activities. The view that science will find the answers to environmental problems reflects the 'realist' view of science, which is the belief that science literally describes nature.[1] In this realist perspective, repeatable experiments on particular and isolatable parts of natural systems, including particles, genes and cells, provide the knowledge base on which science is said to proceed. Hence most science research funding is directed towards 'pure' science, and especially physics, molecular biology and genetics. This kind of science is essentially reductionist for it works on parts of the natural world in isolation from other parts, the operative assumption being that it is possible to build up a picture of the totality of nature by isolating and working on particular instances of atomic, cellular and genetic structure.

The study of climate change

The study of climate change is a case in point. In the 1970s, as Bryan Wynne points out, British meteorological science was exclusively focused on the kind of climate research which was amenable to 'analytical atomization, high precision and single variable measurement and manipulation'.₁ A new centre of climate research was established at the University of East Anglia to study long-term climate change in history – for example by correlating records of crop production with ice core samples taken from the poles, indicating mean temperatures and carbon dioxide levels, and extrapolating from such studies possible future climatic change patterns and cycles. This approach represented such a radical departure from conventional climate science that the new centre was refused funding by public science funding agencies. Eventually it attracted private funding from an oil company.

Under pressure from environmentalists about changing weather patterns and the possible contribution of human carbon production, scientists have now adopted more systemic and complex approaches to studying the earth's climate. The IPCC began to develop supercomputer climate models which included a whole raft of factors in the endeavour to determine the possible effects, both locally and globally, of climate heating. But even these models excluded certain key processes and elements such as the interaction between cloud formation and solar radiation, or the carbon-absorbing potential of increasing populations of oceanic algae.[1] But the most important processes which were excluded from the IPCC model were the social processes which determine the quantities of carbon and other greenhouse gases such as methane produced in different areas of the globe. Physical processes such as methane or carbon accumulation in the upper atmosphere are driven as much by the outcomes of complex political and economic arrangements, systems and relationships in human society as they are by interactions in natural systems.[2]

Twenty years ago most climatologists discounted the possibility of humanly generated climate change because it was assumed human activity could not fundamentally affect weather patterns. We now know this is not so and scientists have adopted alternative models. Social pressure on scientists to use their skills to explore climate change forced a change in the metaphors and models through which scientists examined and described climate and ultimately led to the adoption of a new paradigm of climate change which admitted human activities such as fossil fuel burning, deforestation and animal domestication as key variables within the paradigm. The socially generated motives for the adoption of a new paradigm is a good example of Thomas Kuhn's now classic account of the social processes which influence scientific research, The Structure of Scientific Revolutions.[3] The paradigm shift in climatology is evidenced in the second assessment report of the IPCC, which devotes considerable attention to the socio-political factors which influence climate change and in which the IPCC proposes international mechanisms for trading carbon emission permits as one approach to dealing with the socio-political dimensions of global climate change.[4]

What has happened to the study of climate change is in many ways a fitting metaphor for the role of science in the environmental crisis. Natural science operates in a reductive way on particular elements in natural systems, elements which are often isolated from their wider environment while under study. This mode of operation excludes interactions between different elements in the field, with the consequence that physics or molecular biology and ecology are often in conflict. This method also of course excludes the human observer, with the consequence that human and social interactions with physical processes are often excluded from the procedures by which technologies – the outcomes of scientific research – are constructed and exploited.

This reductive approach may be part of the reason why scientific narratives of the environmental crisis seem to lack the power to change human behaviour. Most politicians in the European Union (EU) agree that global warming is at least partly a consequence of human activity. Few politicians in the USA though are prepared to accept this possibility, and the public dissemination of the science of climate change in the

USA involves the repeated claim that this conclusion is still open to scientific disconfirmation. Hence at the most recent climate conventions at Kyoto and Brazil, the USA preferred to enter into agreements to trade its carbon production against reductions in other nations' carbon production rather than agree to real reductions in its own consumption of fossil fuels, even though the people of the USA, who represent 5% of global population, produce 60% of the global carbon output.

Underlying social processes

We cannot avoid then an examination of the social processes which underlie global environmental discourse, including scientific discourse. And as soon as we do this, fundamental issues of human ethics and international justice arise. If the IPCC is to be believed, carbon consumption in the North equates to increased hurricanes, rising sea levels, increasing unpredictability of monsoons creating both extremes of drought and flood in different regions (such as we saw in the wake of El Nino over the past two years), uncontrollable forest fires in some regions, including Amazon and Indonesia, and uncontrollable and unprecedented flooding in others, including Bangladesh.

The residents of the USA and the EU are so far not seriously affected by growing climate unpredictability. Degrees of industrialisation and consumer comfort in these Northern regions rely upon high energy use, seventy or eighty times that of energy use in the South, whereas the consequences of this energy use are visited primarily on individuals and communities in the South. The majority of individuals in the North may be inconvenienced by climate change; they may even pay slightly more for their buildings insurance because of the growing frequency of floods and high winds. However, few communities in the North will collectively experience a declining quality of life because of climate change. The exception may be residents of the hurricane-prone areas of the south-eastern states of the USA. However, the availability of publicly subsidised insurance against hurricane damage for householders, farmers and businesses in these states actually encourages settlement in hurricane- prone areas. Loss of life remains a risk, but the Federal government insures and subsidises settlement in hurricane areas for social reasons.

Social processes in the North sustain profligate patterns of energy use which reflect the interests of Northern corporations, and to a lesser extent consumers, and which do not factor into the price of energy the human and ecological impact of excessive energy consumption in other parts of the world. Space heating and transportation are the two most significant forms of energy use. Social choices about the technologies of space heating and transport are outcomes of a range of factors including market prices and taxes on fuel; levels of subsidy for different energy production technologies; government regulation of industrial, commercial and domestic building; the provision and convenience of competing transport infrastructures; and urban and rural planning as it affects travel to work, and increasingly travel to shop, patterns.

The two dominant forms of energy use – space heating and transport – are closely interconnected. Choices about the proximity of the workplace to the home have energy implications for working life and leisure. Such choices are again the outcome of planning and commercial decisions as well as individual preference. Taxation has significant effects on both kinds of energy use. Effective and safe public transportation requires public investment which many cities in the UK and the USA are unable to provide because of reductions in property and corporation taxes, and the current policy bias towards taxes on labour – income and national insurance taxes (or payroll) taxes – rather than taxes on energy use, or taxes on machines such as cars, lorries, planes, boilers or computers. Similarly the profligate spread of air travel as the increasingly dominant mode of business and tourist travel, and its growing use in food transportation, is driven by the global zero tax regime on kerosene (air fuel), as contrasted with fuel taxes on petrol and diesel (though gasoline taxes in the USA remain very low), and government subsidies to airport development and the associated infrastructure of airports, motorways and train connections in continental Europe and North America.

The social processes by which technologies are developed, chosen and used are also driven by a combination of government and corporate decision-making which establishes the framework in which consumers make rational choices. The flow of research funds to some technologies – most notably nuclear power and road transport infrastructure – and the lack of funds for others, including alternatives to carbon-burning internal combustion engines such as electric buses and taxis powered by renewably sourced electricity, local heat and light production in small-scale energy schemes, point of consumption utilisation of photoelectric cell solar electricity production, insulation of domestic homes and commercial spaces, integration of work and domestic space, low energy light bulbs, and wind, wave and solar power.

Anti-environmentalists, and especially corporate and consumer lobbies, tend to view a shift in taxation and planning decisions towards environmental sustainability as involving the subversion of economic freedom and consumer choice. In relation to economic freedom, Robert Nozick argues that this is the only human right which nations should seek to enshrine in their constitutions as from it follow all the other rights.[5] However, climate change studies provide evidence that the exercise by one political community of economic freedom in relation to the production and consumption of energy has impacts on the freedoms of other political communities because the earth's atmosphere presents a physical limit as a waste sink to the waste products of energy consumption. In this context political structures which in one country give absolute priority to economic freedom may in other countries produce a situation where the freedom to live is increasingly scarce. In relation to consumer choice, we may observe that consumer choice is already driven by social as much as market mechanisms. For example in relation to the freedom to drive a car, without publicly subsidised roads, public subsidies to traffic police, traffic wardens, to hospitals and ambulances to deal with casualties and deaths, public subsidies in the form of tax breaks for oil exploration, 'private' cars – a misnomer of course – would not be viable. Similarly the large-scale corporate takeover of railways and rolling stock by bus companies in the USA in the 1920s and 1930s, and public decisions to cut rail provision and subsidy in the UK in the 1960s, and again in the 1990s, both had the outcome of greatly increased private car and road freight use. The EU is currently developing a trans European motorway network from northern Scotland to southern and eastern Europe. The European Commission, like the UK government, continues to deploy the great majority of its transport civil servants on road planning and use.

Costs of climate change

Social processes – corporate, bureaucratic and consumer decisions about technology deployment – are critical factors in environmental change. But of course these local social processes are connected with larger social processes, and in particular with global economic and trading arrangements between nation states, and between North and South. The majority of the environmental costs of energy use, historic and current, are borne by tropical and sub-tropical regions, which are much more climate sensitive than the former boreal forests of the temperate zones and are at greater risk of serious disturbance from global climate change and climate heating. Europeans have settled in most of the temperate zones in the Southern as well as the Northern hemisphere, including temperate zones in southern Africa, South America and the Antipodes. Tropical zones are still largely inhabited by peoples whose economic activities involve low energy use and very limited industrialisation compared with the temperate zones. Peoples in most tropical and sub-tropical countries –

Rwanda, Central African Republic, Mozambique, Bangladesh, Pakistan, Jamaica, Haiti, Cuba – experience widespread poverty. All of these countries are also heavily indebted to Northern banks and governments and their economies are subject to control by Northern bankers, which tends to increase the proportion of land devoted to commercial monocrop agriculture for export, which subverts local food security and encourages more forest clearance, with further impacts upon local climate change. Certain tropical countries such as Brazil, Malaysia and Indonesia have seen more development, but the development is very unequal and has been characterised by widespread environmental abuse and especially deforestation. A second major feature of the environmental crisis – tropical deforestation – is therefore connected to the first – energy consumption and global warming.

The historic transfer of resources from tropical to temperate regions continues today in the guise of free trade and capital deregulation. This means that the costs of climate change are borne disproportionately by tropical zones and that they are in effect subsidising the high levels of energy use in temperate regions. The global situation with respect to climate change is analogous to the regional impact of acid rain, which is exported via the prevailing winds from the sulphur valley of southeast Yorkshire to the forests and fjords of Scandinavia.

In addition to the climate change effects of energy use in the North, we should recall that much of the energy consumed in the North is itself at the price of direct environmental and human abuses in the South, as shown by the deleterious impacts of oil prospecting, extraction and refining on environments and communities in countries such as Nigeria and Columbia, where oil companies have employed private armies or colluded with government military to defend their installations against local communities who have been blighted by poor environmental standards. The Northern appetite for oil also fuels continuing geopolitical conflict in the

Middle East where widespread human rights abuses and anti-democratic government are sustained by the flow of arms and capital investment from the West as part of the bargain which keeps the oil flowing and keeps the oil price down.

The global environment connects us all, but the global economy is managed and sustained in ways which do not take cognisance of the global or local environmental costs of different kinds of economic activity and trade, nor of the absorbative limits of natural sinks for the waste products of industrial processes.

Is there an answer?

Is there an answer? If it is to be found in the sciences, it is not in the natural sciences but the social sciences. Available technologies are already capable of producing energy needs from renewable sources, though perhaps not at current levels of temperate country energy use. The problem is not a technological one but an economic and political one. Money values attached to energy products in global markets do not reflect the human or environmental costs of production or consumption of energy, or of goods produced using different kinds of energy. The dissociation of money from fixed assets and political communities is an important and related part of this problem – what Baudrillard calls the hyper-reality of international finance.[6] Equally, trading and financial structures which engender the continuing postcolonial coercion of natural resources, including land, minerals, forests or fisheries, from subsistence farmers, fisherfolk and tribal peoples, who still comprise more than 80% of the world's food producers, contribute to the unequal environmental impacts of the 'economic freedoms' exercised by Northern producers and consumers.

Economics is the social science most implicated in environmental decision making, and in the unequal and unjust exchange of poor peoples' environments for rich nations unsustainable consumption. But academic economists and practitioners alike have adopted a neoclassical model of economic activity which discounts human and environmental factors and trusts to so-called 'laws of supply and demand' and 'rational choice theory'. The dominant theory of markets fails to take account of the human social construction of money value itself, and of public goods such as infrastructure without which there would be far fewer rational choices to be made by consumers and producers alike. Equally it fails to take account of the constraints on economic or market activity represented by the biophysical environment. This is a failing of *all* neoclassical economists, both capitalist and Marxist. They all treat the economic system as a sphere of value creation which is independent of natural systems. Even natural scarcity is said to be a social construct, indeed the desired aim of market actors, for scarcity – either symbolic or by cornering the market – raises the price and hence the added value of a product.

Ecological economists argue that the human value economy is a sub-system of the physical economy.[7] Money is not independent of land but deeply intertwined with it. When corporations and banks create money values through stock markets, bank credits or hedge funds, they create not just a hyper-real electronic system of money value transfer but bank deposits in search of production opportunities. Ultimately the productive use of money requires physical factors such as land as well as labour and machinery. Most of the land which is currently mobilised by exponentially accumulating money values in Northern economies is in the South. Similarly, waste sinks increasingly impact on the South, both in respect of climate change and warming, but also as the South becomes the waste dump for Northern toxic production, either by the direct export of toxic waste or by the export of dirty technologies to countries with low labour costs and low environmental regulation.

One obvious and rational solution to many environmental problems in the North which utilises market mechanisms and is beginning to be embraced by some neoclassical economists, particularly in Europe, is environmental taxation. But the increasingly global character of the economy makes ecological taxation more problematic. Carbon taxes, or even petrol taxes, are resisted by business and commercial interests, and the politicians they frequently fund, because they reduce the competitiveness of Northern producers relative to Southern producers. The corporate lobby is resistant to the environmentalist riposte that Southern competitiveness is undermined by climate change generated by profligate energy use in the North. The peoples and economies of Bangladesh, Nicaragua and Honduras have all been recently devastated by rare extremes of climate in 1998 which climatologists believe are linked to global warming and hence to Northern energy consumption. If the North will not compensate the South for such effects, nor effectively reduce its profligate energy consumption, what other mechanisms are there for the realisation of global environmental justice?

Divine law and environmental rights

Distributive justice

I have argued elsewhere that the Hebrew Bible indicates that divine commandments have cosmic and not just human and social significance.[8] A central principle of Hebrew law is that of distributive justice. This principle is applied primarily within the household of Israel. Where the rich accrue to themselves too much of the land and its products they are said to contravene the law of God because their greed denies the poor their due participation in the abundance of the land (Isaiah 3:13–15). In Israelite society, the law was the key mechanism for the balancing of the interests of rich and poor. The Sabbath and Jubilee laws provided for periodic redistribution of excess wealth, creating an obligation on the rich and successful to bring back the poor, indebted and unsuccessful into full membership, as landowners, of the household of Israel (Leviticus 25).⁹ In addition to creating an obligation for the wealthy, the Hebrew Bible in places indicates a correlative right of the poor to receive their due. Thus Isaiah condemns those who in his day were writing the needs of the poor out of the law because they thereby 'turn aside the needy from justice' and 'rob the poor of my people of their right (*mishpat*)' (Isaiah 10:2). Jeremiah also speaks of those scoundrels who 'take over the goods of others', who 'have become great and rich': 'they do not judge with justice the cause of the orphan, to make it prosper, and they do not defend the rights (*mishpat*) of the needy' (Jeremiah 5:28).

The balance of wealth and land between Israel and her neighbours was also said to have been subject to divine will, though not to specific provisions of the law. However, when through military prowess or economic success Israel succeeded in outdoing her neighbours, prophets warned her rulers that they were buying earthly security and power at the price of spiritual probity and divine favour. Amos and Jeremiah, like the historians of the book of Kings, regarded the military and trading successes of some of Israel's later rulers as a cause of divine disapprobation and ultimately of conquest and exile. The provisions of the law were in any case not limited to the people of Israel. Aliens and animals also came within its purview. Foreigners who dwelt in the land of Israel were said to have certain economic claims upon Israelite farmers, and farmers were not to farm so much of the land that wild animals had no undomesticated land in which to live and roam. Similarly, the consequences of human disobedience of the laws of God are not limited to the people of Israel. The fertility of the land and of animals, and even the climate, are said to be affected by Israel's abandonment of the just distribution of nature's wealth.[10]

Distributive justice and rights between nations are both at issue in relation to global climate change and the costs and benefits of the mobilisation and use of particular energy sources and technologies. Some environmental economists argue that taxation and public subsidy regimens should reflect the international as well as the local and regional costs of technology and energy use. In particular they say that energy for space heating, industrial production and transportation should be priced according to the global as well as the local environmental impacts of its production and use, and not just the economic costs of production. However, the intractable problem is how to factor in international costs. As we have seen, the USA resists environmental controls on its own transportation systems arising from the costs of climate change which, within its own borders, the USA is capable of meeting.

Analogously the EU resists 'economic' and environmental migrants, though it encourages the free movement of natural resources and capital. Inward trade in cut flowers, exotic vegetables and fruits is linked with the increasing flow of migrants from South to North because land which is used for export crops was formerly used for subsistence farming. Poor farmers are driven onto marginal lands and forests, or into urban shantytowns. Marginal land erosion and desertification as well as climate change are all major contributors to the growing problem of environmental refugees.

Since the publication in 1991 of the Brundtland Commission Report, *Our Common Future*, a growing body of international environmental treaty advances the case for the creation of global mechanisms that give expression to international distributive justice with regard to the global environment. The Brundtland report used the language of rights as a means to give expression to the universality of the moral claims raised by the biophysical limits to the environment: 'All human beings have the fundamental right to an environment adequate for their health and well being.'[11] Legal systems in thirty countries now recognise the existence of environmental rights, thus at least in principle allowing individuals and communities to sue corporations and public institutions for environmental damage.[12]

The extension of the legal recognition of environmental rights would not resolve all global environmental conflicts. It is also an admittedly anthropocentric procedure, though it may be that the recognition of the human right to an environment which promotes flourishing will contribute to the spread of the idea of the rights of other living beings to an environment which promotes their flourishing also. The recognition of human environmental rights both nationally and internationally is only one element in the global quest for environmental justice and the rebalancing of the environmental rights of individuals and communities with the economic and bureaucratic powers of corporations and nation states. But its advocates in the United Nations (UN) and elsewhere contend that it would offer a surer ground for arbitrating between the powerful and the powerless than some other forms of arbitration of international environmental conflicts. However there are a number of problems with this approach to global environmental justice; there is space here to deal with only two. The first is the question of whether human rights in general, and environmental rights in particular, are a theologically and ethically appropriate way for Christians to speak about environmental justice, and whether by commending this approach we are not in fact evading the true source of the problem and hence failing to commend the right response. The second is whether constitutional recognition of environmental rights in particular nations will enhance environmental justice in an increasingly global economy.

Should Christians embrace the idea of environmental rights?

Christian theologians were not quick to recognise the legitimacy of rights talk. Its earliest advocates were not theologians but political philosophers such as Tom Paine and Jean Jacques Rousseau who were regarded by ecclesiastics as heretics. And it was those modern states which were most avowedly secular in their revolutionary origination – France and the USA – which first enshrined individual rights in national constitutions. And therein is part of the problem some theologians and philosophers have with rights talk.

Rights in scripture

By speaking of certain rights as inalienable, such as the right to life, liberty or property, or the right to a decent environment, modern advocates of human rights make claims about the human condition which arrogate much which Jews and Christians have traditionally ascribed to God and to God's rights over creation, and only derivatively to humans. Rather than conceiving of *mispat* or right as inalienable and original to the human condition, the right referred to in scripture is a right which is derivative on the constitution of persons made in the image of God, on their constitution as beings in the body of God's creation, and on their reconstitution as persons who are being renewed after the image of Jesus Christ who came to restore the sinful inheritance of personhood.

Thus in Hebrew law and in the New Testament the right to property is not an absolute right but a right derived from God's gift of creation to humans and, in the case of the Israelites, God's gift of the promised land to the former Hebrew slaves. Limits on the rights and freedoms of property holders, such as the Sabbath and Jubilee laws, were an expression of the fact that the property holders were not absolute owners of the land but stewards or tenants who held it in trust on behalf of God who gave it to them. Similarly the right to a due share in God's creation for all persons, and not just property holders, is derived from God's original gifting of creation to the descendants of the first man and the first woman, and hence to all the peoples of the earth. The right to liberty is even more clearly a derivative right. According to the laws of the Hebrew Bible, freedom is not to be expressed in such a way as to oppress the poor, and according to the Apostle Paul freedom is also constrained by the possibility that exercising it may give offence to the brethren.

Rights as an expression of autonomy

The distinctiveness of modern rights talk is not the concept or claim of right. This is very ancient. It is rather, as Oliver O'Donovan points out, the idea that human rights are original, 'a primitive endowment of power with which the subject first engages with society' rather than derivative on the sovereignty and justice of God.[13] In other words, modern human rights are at best an expression of the autonomy of modern societies and modern persons from dependence on God. But at worst, as Stanley Hauerwas argues, they represent a denial of the sovereignty of God and the original rights of God over God's creation and all that lives within it, including persons made in the image of God.[14] Rights talk arrogates too much to the human, thereby substituting human claims to earthly sovereignty for the ultimate claims of the sovereign God over God's creation. Indeed this is the central *theological* characteristic of the modern scientistic project to transform the diversity and alterity of God's creation into the service of human needs and aspirations. And in this denial of the divine ordering of creation to God and to all God's creatures, and not just to humans, we may identify the true root of our current environmental crisis. Surely then it is quixotic to adopt the language of rights, a language which seems to involve the denial of divine sovereignty, as a means for restraining this technological remaking of creation.

Rights designed to restrain conflict

There is a further problem with rights talk: the tendency of rights talk to construct human relations as essentially characterised by conflict rather than peace. In *Perpetual Peace* Immanuel Kant, one of the foremost modern advocates of rights discourse, argued that whereas republican states may achieve peace within their borders through a social contract which affirms and balances the rights to liberty of all citizens, nation states which are not in federal relationships with each other do not enjoy such a shared contract and are consequently in a state of perpetual conflict or hostility even if they are not actually at war. In order to restrain such conflict and to realise international peace between nations Kant argues that a minimal recognition be given to the rights of all persons by virtue of their human nature, rather than of their citizenship of particular nations. Federations between nations may therefore be realised which advance the cause of international peace by this mutual, if minimal, recognition of the rights accruing to all human beings.[15]

In the Kantian conception of human society then, human life is constituted by inherent conflict which rights talk, social contracts and other liberal political procedures must restrain, but cannot undo. Against this approach, John Millbank argues that liberal notions of liberty and rights, arising as they do from a conflictual model of human life, must be rejected by Christians because they affirm the essentially modern and atheistic understanding of humanness as the quest for power and ownership, and of social theory as the means for arbitrating the inherently conflictual nature of this quest. In the light of the Gospel, human life is not fundamentally a conflictual quest for power or ownership, but rather a quest for union with the source of all power, which is God himself, and a quest not to own but to be owned by God.

> 'One could say that Christianity denies ontological necessity to sovereign rule and absolute ownership. And that it seeks to recover the concealed text of an original peaceful creation beneath the palimpsest of the negative distortion of *dominium*, through the superimposition of a third redemptive template, which corrects these distortions by means of forgiveness and atonement.'[16]

Millbank in this crucial if slightly obscure paragraph points of course to the deeply theological character of our modern environmental crisis. The sinful distortion of dominion is at the heart of our abuse of the creation. Its resolution may only be found in our repentance of the sin of the will to power over nature and over others, and our recovery of a sense of the

Lordship of Christ over God's creation, in which recovery alone can we and the creation hope for that peaceable kingdom in which animals and humans walk the earth without fear of each other as once they are said to have done before the Flood.

Using the language of rights

Now I, and perhaps some of you, have no difficulty in agreeing with Stanley Hauerwas and John Millbank when they contend that beneath the modern rhetoric of rights and the modern practices of politics and economics lies a darker reality of violence and conflict, of rich nations and corporations treading down poor nations and communities, a reality whose roots lie in our collective denial of the sovereignty of God over creation, and which secular liberal rhetoric and political arrangements are capable of obscuring but incapable of redeeming.[17] But as Christians who are concerned about the environment we cannot avoid engaging in some fashion with secular politics and economics, for it is in this sphere of the secular that the weak are downtrodden and the environment is abused. The problem with Millbank and Hauerwas' principled theological rejection of engagement with liberal political arrangements for the arbitration of the kinds of conflicts which underlie our current difficulties over climate change is that we Christians still have to live in a political and economic system – global capitalism – which does, for the most part, deny the rights of God over creation, and which construes the human use of creation in terms of conflict for scarce resources rather than mutual enjoyment and sharing of the original goodness and abundance of the derived wealth of God's creation.

As Christians we aspire to live in worshipping communities in which there is no need for talk of rights, in which the stronger give place to the weaker, in which our leaders come among us as our servants, and in which the wealthy freely share with the poor from their abundance. But even in this aspiration we often find our actual social experience of church lets us down. Even more so, our experience of living in nation states which, in the case of this nation state and others like it, still use our taxes to advance our putative interests in employment and economic growth and even international 'security' by subsidising and promoting the sale of weapons of mass destruction and human torture to nations around the globe to the detriment of the environment and human rights.[18]

The problem with the language of rights for Christians is that it is a poor substitute for the recognition of our mutual ontological status as persons made in the image of God, and as living embodied beings who share creaturehood with all other life forms in this cosmos. The language of rights, as Jeffrey Stout argues, is a minimalist language, a kind of moral *pidgin* which is also a secularized mode of public discourse.[19] It does not say all that can or should be said about the conditions of life which make for human flourishing, including most especially the worship and love of God. But even as we name the name of God, and remind the modern world and modern capitalists that by making gods of money and power and consumer goods, they and we are abusing creation precisely because we are idolising the creature rather than the Creator, at the same time we must engage with those people of good will of every faith, including that of secular humanism, who are seeking to instigate arrangements between nations – and in particular between the powerful nations of the formerly Christian North and the weaker nations of the South – which will produce a fairer distribution of the earth's limited resources, including its capacity to absorb the waste products and gases of our consumptive civilisation.

Human rights may not be the language of choice for Christians but it is the characteristic language in the modern world through which victims of torture and their advocates seek to defend themselves against their torturers, in which slaves have won their liberty from bondage, and in which formerly colonised peoples have gained their putative independence from their colonisers. Millbank and Hauerwas give us a powerful account of what it is to be Christian in a world which is not Christian. But they are less helpful in constructing those collective social arrangements which Christians, and Christian environmentalists, may pursue with others who wish to recognise, own and preserve the common shared goodness of creation but who are not baptised members of the Christian church.[20]

But even if we do promote rights language as a means for righting global wrongs, including environmental wrongs, we may still note that its minimalism, or thinness, does not serve well the cause of the preservation of the embodied character of the environment and of human flourishing. The original Universal Declaration of Human Rights, which was fifty years old in 1998, has a remarkably unsituated and disembodied account of rights which rarely refers to the biophysical nature of the environment in which we actually pursue our flourishing and experience liberty. Article 3 of the Declaration recognises the right to life, which implicitly includes the right to bodily safety, and Article 25 recognises a right to 'a standard of living adequate for (the) health and well-being'. But these implicit references do not constitute a sound basis for the defence of environmental rights.

The bodily character of human rights

In contrast to the Universal Declaration, Dietrich Bonhoeffer, writing earlier in the 1940s, adopted a language of rights which speaks much more of their embodied character and their relationship to God's creation. Larry Rasmussen notes that Dietrich Bonhoeffer was the first Protestant theologian to use the language of rights, and he points out that Bonhoeffer's adoption of a more embodied language of rights is closely related to his account of the essentially embodied nature of earthly existence.[21] In his commentary on the early chapters of Genesis, *Creation and Fall*, Bonhoeffer says that 'the essential point of human existence is its bond with mother earth, its being as body'.[22]

And he continues,

> 'The human body is distinguished from all non-human bodies by being the existence- form of God's Spirit on earth, as it is wholly undifferentiated from all other life by being of this earth. The human body really only lives by God's Spirit; this is indeed its essential nature. God glorifies himself in the body: in this specific form of the human body. For this reason God enters into the body again where the original in its created being has been destroyed. He enters it in Jesus Christ.'[23]

For Bonhoeffer salvation is an essentially embodied event which has implications for all embodied life in the cosmos, as well as for the embodiment of all humans within the cosmos, and the image of God which is restored in Jesus Christ is an essentially embodied image.[24] In his incomplete and posthumously published *Ethics* Bonhoeffer goes on to argue that humans have 'a right to bodily life' for 'the living human body is always the person himself/herself'.[25] As Rasmussen puts it,

> 'Natural rights, then, reside in bodily requirements and bodily integrity. That which is necessary for bodily flourishing – and that certainly includes its protection against violation – merits a right secured in law. These rights are grounded in creation itself and belong to life's requirements for flourishing, since our bodiliness is our unbreakable bond with earth and all its creatures.'[26]

Modern Catholic social teaching reflects this same concern of Bonhoeffer's with the bodily character of human rights. As Pope John declares in *Pacem in Terris*, 'we see that every man has the right to life, to bodily integrity, and to the means which are suitable for the proper development of life'.[27] Since more than 80% of the world's farmers are subsistence farmers, we can see that the provision of the means suitable for human development must include, for the poor, if not for the rich who buy their food in supermarkets, a stable environment in which to grow food. Under economic rights, *Pacem in Terris* refers to the right to 'working conditions in which physical health is not endangered'.[30] Both these rights recognise the importance of environment and of respect for the embodied condition of human flourishing.

Sustenance rights

Among contemporary Protestant theologians Nicholas Wolterstorff has given a more coherent account of the theological origins and character of rights than any other. Like Bonhoeffer, he also wishes to emphasise the crucial import of the material nature of human rights, and in particular of what he calls sustenance rights. In *Until Justice and Peace Embrace* he argues that the right to sustenance is one of the most fundamental of all human rights, and more fundamental than the right to freedom of speech or property rights.[28] However he also notes that the modern West, and in particular the USA, is much less willing to recognise the right of a person to sufficient sustenance than their right to complain publicly about not having sustenance. Wolterstorff understands sustenance rights as 'a claim on our fellow human beings to social arrangements that ensure that we will be adequately sustained in existence.' In other words, the possession of this right creates responsibilities for individuals and groups not to threaten the sustenance of other individuals or groups. The recognition of this right requires a social guarantee which involves the collective recognition of 'correlative duties' in the avoidance of threats to other peoples' sustenance. For Wolterstorff this way of seeing sustenance rights relates not just to natural law (as do the rights in *Pacem in Terris*, for example) but to divinely revealed law in the Bible which indicates God's particular concern for those whose sustenance is threatened,

> 'Seeing that rights are claims to guarantees against threats makes clear that rights are God's charter for the weak and defenceless ones in society. A right is the legitimate claim for protection of those too weak to help themselves. It is the legitimate claim of the defenceless against the more devastating and common of life's threats which, at that time and place, are remediable. It is the claim of the little ones in society to restraint upon

> economic and political and physical forces that would otherwise be too strong for them to resist.'[29]

Wolterstorff argues that the claim of the right to sustenance is a claim that arises from the divine ordering of the creation, part of the natural endowment of every person who is made in the image of God. It is in other words a natural right. But it is also a theological right which is affirmed by the redemptive purposes of God for fallen human society as revealed both in the laws of the Old Testament, which were designed to distribute nature's wealth through social arrangements which ensured that the poor received the natural endowment, and in the revelation of Jesus Christ who reaffirmed in his teaching and in the values he inculcated in his followers the central place of the poor in the redemptive purposes of God as manifested in his incarnation, death and resurrection. Thus Wolterstorff's account roots the origins and character of rights in natural law, in divine revelation, and in the practices of Israelite and Christian communities.

In the modern world, Wolterstorff argues, threats to sustenance have become commonplace, especially in the 'Third World', and these threats are closely connected with economic, political and social structures in 'the West', as well as the Third World, and with global trading and economic arrangements which are largely controlled by the West. For Wolterstorff therefore the recognition of the right to sustenance involves Christians and others of good will in efforts to reform the policies, in particular the foreign and trading policies, of Western nations so as to remove these threats.

Will environmental rights enhance justice in a global economy?

As we have seen, the threats to bodily life and sustenance represented by climatic change in many very poor countries are often ignored by Northern governments which neglect, or refuse to recognise, often under strong pressure from domestically headquartered multinational corporations, the duties which these threats involve for the most profligate generators of greenhouse gases. The incorporation of environmental rights into national constitutions will go some way to providing a legal basis for the defence of the environments of persons and communities whose safety and sustenance is threatened by climate change or other forms of pollution, particularly by corporations domiciled in countries which recognise these rights. The recognition of the environmental rights of individuals and local communities is all the more important in the light of the growing ascription of rights to corporations in national and international law and treaty, without corresponding duties. Corporations have already acquired the right to be treated as fictive persons in North American and European courts. Currently transnational corporations and governments in the North are involved in the construction of a new body of international law around the World Trade Organization, the North American Free Trade Agreement (NAFTA), the EU and the recently shelved Multilateral Agreement on Investment, which will raise the legal claims of such fictive persons above those of local communities of persons and above political entities such as nation states.[30]

The recognition of environmental rights, as a sub-category of economic or sustenance rights, also has crucial implications for the foreign as well as domestic policies of the richest nations and federations of nations, in particular the USA, Japan and the EU, as one of the most prominent rights philosophers in the USA, Henry Shue, recognises in his *Basic Rights: Subsistence, Affluence and U.S. Foreign Policy*.[31] It has even clearer implications for any nation which claims, as the UK currently does, that it espouses an ethical foreign policy. Such an espousal, in the light of the threats to basic existence in the South represented by Northern- originated climate change, requires radical changes in UK domestic policies, and in particular in energy policy, if it is to be more than public relations rhetoric, changes of the kind which the current government, like the former, shows little inclination to make in relation to transport policy, green taxation and energy conservation.

However, in a global economic order where many corporate actors are wealthier and more powerful than many nations, particularly those in the South, a new international recognition of environmental rights and their affirmation in international and legally binding treaty is also required if global environmental injustices are to begin to be redressed. In recognition of the global character of the forces which undermine local environments and their capacity to sustain human life and flourishing, the UN Commission on Human Rights now advocates the extension of international recognition of human rights to include the right to a healthy environment.[32] This extension of the international recognition of human rights will also require the establishment of an international court with internationally recognised powers of judicial and economic sanction if it is genuinely to contribute to reduced conflict over environmental resources. In such a court, holders of newly recognised environmental rights would be able to take their case against those nations and corporations whose environmental abuses genuinely threaten their human sustenance and flourishing. In the light of experience with extensions of rights language in other spheres, we may reasonably anticipate that the very existence of such an international treaty and court will encourage, in a way environmentalist exhortation and international environmental conferences have not yet succeeded in doing, a much more radical shift in consumption patterns and energy use in the rich North. Until such a shift comes about, environmentalists in the South will continue to regard international environmental discourses and treaties as efforts by the already developed and wealthy nations in the North to hold back the development and standard of living of nations in the South.

Christian critics of rights language argue that it is a poor substitute for relations of love such as those which grace, and not law, prescribe for Christians. However, divine love, as well as divine law, is characterised in the Bible as promoting the interests of the weak over the strong. As Karl Barth put it in a passage from the *Church Dogmatics* cited by Wolterstorff,

> 'the human righteousness required by God and established in obedience – the righteousness which according to Amos 5:24 should pour down as a mighty stream – has necessarily the character of a vindication of right in favour of the threatened innocent, the oppressed poor, widows, orphans and aliens.'[33]

The international and national recognition of environmental rights will have the divinely legitimated effect of promoting the interests of the weak over the strong. Inasmuch as nation states and corporations already are accorded the rights of persons, the international recognition of the environmental rights of the environmentally poor may be said to give legal expression to the ideal of divine love as revealed in the incarnation of Jesus Christ and so memorably expressed by Mary his mother: 'He has brought down the powerful from their thrones and lifted up the lowly' (Luke 1: 52).

Notes

1. Wynne, B. 'Scientific knowledge and the global environment' in Redclift, M. and Benton, T. (eds) *Social Theory and the Global Environment*, London: Routledge, 1994, 169–189.
2. Benton, T. and Redclift, M. 'Introduction' in Redclift, M. and Benton, T. (eds) *Social Theory and the Global Environment*, London: Routledge, 1994, 13–14.
3. Kuhn, T.S. *The Structure of Scientific Revolutions*, Chicago: Chicago University Press, 1962.
4. See further Bruce, J.P., Lee, H. Haites, E.F. (eds) *Climate Change 1995: Economic and Social Dimensions of Climate Change. Contribution of Working Group III to the Second Assessment Report of the Intergovernmental Panel on Climate Change*, Cambridge: Cambridge University Press, 1996.
5. Nozick, R. *Anarchy, State and Utopia* ... Oxford: Blackwell, 1974.
6. Baudrillard, J. *The Consumer Society: Myths and Structures*, London: Sage, 1997.
7. Daley, H. *Beyond Growth: The Economics of Sustainable Development*, Boston: Beacon Press, 1996.
8. Northcott, M.S. *The Environment and Christian Ethics*, Cambridge: Cambridge University Press, 1996, chapter 5.
9. See further Christopher Wright's account of these laws and their operation in Wright, C.J.H. *God's People in God's Land: Family, Land and Property in the Hebrew Bible*, Exeter: Paternoster Press, 1990.
10. See further Northcott, M.S. *The Environment and Christian Ethics*, Cambridge: Cambridge University Press, 1996, chapter 5.

11. World Commission on Environment and Development, *Our Common Future*, Oxford: Oxford University Press, 1991, 348.
12. Hayward, T. 'Constitutional environmental rights: a case for political analysis' in *Political Studies* (in press).
13. O'Donovan, O. *The Desire of Nations: Rediscovering the Roots of Political Theology*, Cambridge: Cambridge University Press, 1996, 248.
14. Hauerwas, S. *After Christendom: How the Church is to Behave if Freedom, Justice, and a Christian Nation Are Bad Ideas*, Nashville: Abingdon Press, 1991, chapter 2.
15. Dower, N. *World Ethics: The New Agenda*, Edinburgh: Edinburgh University Press, 1998, 77.
16. Millbank, J. *Theology and Social Theory*, Oxford: Blackwell, 1990, especially chapter 12.
17. For a good representation of Stanley Hauerwas' thought in relation to liberal political arrangements, including rights talk, see his *After Christendom* and also *Despatches from the Front*.
18. It is a little known fact that a large proportion of the debt owed to the British treasury by poor nations in the South has arisen as a consequence of export credit guarantees provided by the Department of Trade and Industry for the sale of arms to poor nations in the South. See further Northcott, M. *Life After Debt: Christianity and Global Justice*, London: SPCK, 1999.
19. Stout, J. *Ethics After Babel: The Languages of Morals and their Discontents*, Cambridge: James Clarke, 1988, 80.
20. In an interesting aside Hauerwas owns 'I make no pretense to think about the moral life for those who do not share in the baptism made possible by Christ's death and resurrection' in *Despatches from the Front*, p. 230, n. 19.
21. Rasmussen, L. *Earth Community, Earth Ethics*, Maryknoll: Orbis Books, 1996.
22. Bonhoeffer, D. *Creation and Fall: A Theological Interpretation of Genesis 1–3*, 45, cited in Rasmussen, L. *Earth Community, Earth Ethics*, Maryknoll: Orbis Books, 1996, 309.
23. Ibid, 46.
24. Rasmussen, L. *Earth Community, Earth Ethics*, Maryknoll: Orbis Books, 1996, 308.
25. Bonhoeffer, *Ethics*, 156 and 183, cited in Rasmussen, L. *Earth Community, Earth Ethics*, Maryknoll: Orbis Books, 1996, 308–309.
26. Ibid, 309.
27. Pope John XXIII, *Pacem in Terris: Peace on Earth*, London: Catholic Truth Society, 1963.
28. Wolterstorff, N. *Until Justice and Peace Embrace*, Grand Rapids, MI: Eerdmans, 1983, 82.
29. Ibid, 84.
30. Under the terms of NAFTA the Canadian government had to pay more than 200 million dollars compensation to a US corporation which wished to import a particularly toxic and carcinogenic petroleum additive into Canada. In trying to prevent this company from importing this toxic substance Canada was found to have infringed the terms of NAFTA.
31. Shue, H. *Basic Rights: Subsistence, Affluence and U.S. Foreign Policy*, Princeton: Princeton University Press, 1981.
32. See further Popovi'c, N. 'In pursuit of environmental human rights: commentary on the Draft Declaration of Principles on Human Rights and the Environment', *Columbia Law Review*, 1996, 27, 3, cited in Hayward, T. 'Constitutional environmental rights: a case for political analysis' in *Political Studies* (in press).
33. Barth, K. *Church Dogmatics*, II, 1, 386, cited in Wolterstorff, N. *Until Justice and Peace Embrace*, Grand Rapids, MI: Eerdmans, 1983, 73.

9 – Christians, environment and society: A response to Michael Northcott

Chris Sugden

> The Revd Dr Chris Sugden is Director of Academic Affairs at the Oxford Centre for Mission Studies
>
> Those in the industrialised North have much to learn from those in the two-thirds world about the missiological relationship between the environment and Christianity.
>
> **Keywords:** environment, creation, fall, poverty, missiology

The environment has become like motherhood and apple-pie. So what might Christians have to contribute specifically to the cause? One well-trodden approach seeks to discover the lowest common denominator on which we can agree with all those of good will in the areas of public policy, and keep separate that area where matters of faith arise, namely personal life and motivation. Christian faith then comes a matter of motivating concern, and the church is hitched to bandwagons that are being driven by others. Another well-worn path affirms that Christian people should be concerned with bringing the gospel to people. Trees and butterflies have a hard time getting the attention and resources of those on this path. In one approach relevance submerges distinctiveness, and in the other distinctiveness leads to irrelevance. Both approaches derive from the separation of the public and private which characterises Western enlightenment society. It is an approach generally foresworn by the church in the Two-Thirds World. So in seeking a missiological relation between the environment and the Christian faith, I will draw on resources from the Two-Thirds World church.

Creation and fall

Concern for the creation of the one God springs off the pages of the Bible, as is well documented by other papers in this issue. God called humanity to exercise shepherdly stewardship as his representative over the creation and to develop it in the context of the family. Men and women together are to 'image' God, in the same way that a king or a statue in the temple 'imaged' the absentee invisible God on the mountain. They are to exercise dominion like God does, in a shepherdly caring way, over his creation; to be fruitful and multiply in the context of the family; to enable everyone to exercise such stewardship and have access to the resources and fruits of creation; and to exercise a qualitatively different care for persons (who were not to be treated as assets) than for plants and animals, which are assets. Christ the perfect image of God, was the paradigm of humanity in relation to creation, and his disciples are to be conformed to his image, and thus become true stewards of creation.

The fall means that the differences which make up the harmony of the creation can easily become divisions. Thus complementary groups become hostile camps: men against women, rich against poor, and humanity against the environment. This is an expression of sin, and the work of the principalities and powers of evil. The work of Christ on the cross overcame sin and these hostilities and was to bring reconciliation throughout creation. So wherever we see reconciliation, brought by Christians or not, we may see the work of God in Jesus Christ which is 'salvific in intent' – signposts to point to Jesus Christ as the source and fulfilment of God's purpose in creation.

Concern for truth

So far so good. But what praxis expresses such commitments? First we may affirm a concern for truth. We believe this is the way it is with the world. So Michael Northcott's paper engages in the time-honoured prophetic process of 'unmasking the powers', showing what is really going in the world. We may disagree on some aspects of the analysis he offers. And I do. For example, from my work as chair of the Traidcraft Foundation Trustees, I know we have investigated the issue of the role of cash crops in a poor economy. We are fairly convinced that cash crops such as tea, coffee and rubber are beneficial to poorer communities and do not undermine food security. We are also convinced that using fuel to transport goods from one part of the world to another in the process of trade is justified in enabling people to access world markets. But because our Christian commitment does not arise out of an ideological analysis of facts, we can disagree on some of these 'interpreted facts' without doubting one another's integrity. Jesus had an ethical ordering principle, of love for God and love for neighbour, and we may order priorities so that 'preserving the environment' does not become a modern day 'Corban', a reason for neglecting the justified claims of our neighbour. The environment is meant to provide livelihoods.

The poor

Secondly, we may affirm that there is a 'bias to the poor' in that the poor should have access to the resources and fruits of the creation to be able to exercise stewardship as a major expression and experience of being human. Michael clearly expresses this. A Christian concern for creation must always be focused on concern for the crown of creation, humanity. Jesus himself argues in this way: God provides for the birds and the flowers, how much more for you. So as Christians we must always resist the difference between humanity and the environment becoming a division between concern for the environment over and against the livelihood of the poor.

The Brundtland Report[1] specially addressed this issue of the potential division between concern for the environment and for the poor by making the following link: the poor live on the most marginal and vulnerable land. They have the heaviest environmental impact, because their sheer weight of numbers tips the marginal land they live on over the edge of serious environmental degradation. The poor therefore threaten the survival of us all, and must be helped in the name of conservation and survival. This argument draws on the self-interest of the north to help the poor, and also blames the victim for the problem by suggesting the poor are messing it up for everyone else.

Now we enter a minefield and will need Ariadne's thread to link the arguments. We may affirm the shared concern to assist the poor to save the environment. But we may so question many of the assumptions on which the Brundtland concern is based as to have to ask whether our concern is the same.

First, those who work closely with the poor tell us that, for example, in South Asia population growth is destroying the environment. To support the burgeoning population, there is no alternative to the large scale 'dirty' industries that produce environmental pollution, both to produce what their societies need and to provide employment. Protecting the environment is therefore seen as a trade off against an increase in poverty. But poverty means more people living on marginal vulnerable land, which produces more environmental degradation. To protect the environment means addressing poverty and this will mean increasing poor people's share of world trade, which will require transport and consumption of their products elsewhere. So we will need to address the issue of population growth.

Second, the Brundtland Report states the problem of the environment and poverty in terms of economic and scientific reductionism. The Two-Thirds World becomes essentially reactive to Western demands to reduce pollution. Their own contribution of awareness of the interdependence of humanity and the environment is marginal. If made, that contribution usually accuses Christian mission of complicity in repressing the cultures and insights of indigenous peoples and their animist faiths. This accusation affirms Western secularist attacks on the church in the name of animist faiths which Western secularists do not affirm for themselves, but do affirm for their devotees in the name of cultural and moral autonomy.

However, poverty cannot be reduced to economics. I would want to go beyond Michael's affirmation that economics is central, as he affirms, or that political economy is central, as his arguments actually seem to suggest. We also need to go beyond the Brundtland notion of blaming the poor. Research and surveys on successful antipoverty projects identify that the crucial issue is the culture of poverty. In the culture of poverty, life is fragile and cheap. There is no hope. People hesitate to take risks because everything is going to be worse than it is at the moment. People cling on to what they have got. They do not think about tomorrow because today is enough of a problem as it is. People have low self esteem. Any attempt to enable people to change such a situation must address the culture of poverty, to enable people to be subjects and not merely objects or even beneficiaries of other people's actions. So we will need to enable people to have self worth as dignified human beings who are called to be stewards of creation. No amount of grants, programmes or projects on their own can provide this.

Third, we must be self-aware about our Western Christian culture as a culture of power with a commitment to techne and law. The need to clean up the effluents of dirty industries in the south and to find alternative sources of energy all speak of the role of techne. The need to regulate powerful multinational corporations by the legal enforcement of environmental rights speaks of a confidence in the rule and role of law. Both commitments stem from a confidence that we have the power to do these things. But significant problems prevent us being too confident as Christians in these approaches. First, Western culture is busy removing the foundations of techne and law. It is techne which has created the problems; can techne be also called on to solve them? Secondly, Western society is moving away from any notion of prescribed behaviour in personal matters, and because of that to more and more prescription in public matters. There is no foundation for required behaviour, so the workplace is becoming more prescriptive with audits and procedures precisely because there is no agreed objective basis for agreed behaviour. On what basis can a culture which increasingly affirms the unfettered right of the individual to self-expression call for extension of legislation about the environment? So the spectre emerges of the powerful Western world imposing its analysis of the problem of the environment and its scientific and legal blueprints based on a worldview which it has itself rejected on the rest of the world in the name of environmental protection as though it knew best how to remedy the situation. It becomes an exercise in sheer power with no visible moral basis.

Humanity and creation

We must therefore revisit the Christian understanding of the relationship between humanity and creation. Many of the solutions that share a supposed common ground between Christians and others of good will in fact share much less than they might suppose. There is a Christian understanding of humanity as persons, different from the rest of creation; of the poor and the nature of poverty; of the moral basis of law and rights. We will have to deal with the first objection to a Christian contribution, namely the accusation that Christians themselves taken part in the oppression of cultures which had a holistic understanding of the relationship of humanity and creation. In short, the considered view of Professor Lamin Sanneh of Yale is that nowhere where Christians have settled in a culture for the long haul have they undermined that culture.[2] Rather the evidence is that in writing down over 180 languages into which they have translated the Bible, Christians have made major contributions to cultural renewal and survival.

We must also take account of the pragmatism in Christian missiology. The New Testament calls the gospel 'good news to the poor'. This means that it must be heard and experienced by the poor as good news to be authentic. We may then ask what is achievable by Christians for the poor through covenant communities (churches)? Does Michael's approach have too much of a grand design about it. It tends to be ahistorical in bringing all aspects of the global environmental crisis together when the crisis has taken different forms over the last 30 years. We no longer hear the cries that we will run out of food or out of renewable resources. The cries about environmental waste are rather recent. Michael's approach also tends to be well ahead of public opinion in the West in asking for legal enforcement of environmental rights. It tends to ignore the small incremental steps and priorities that have to be chosen to make a difference.

Practical Christian missiology

May I therefore bring together some of those choices and steps that might illumine a practical Christian missiology that links Christian faith, the environment and the poor. First, the Christian church is the largest non-governmental organisation in the world. It is the world's most effective deliverer of health. It is also the organisation closest to the poor since the vast majority of its members are poor. These are the observations of the president of the World Bank and of the World Health Organisation. Smart international organisations are beginning to recognise this and to see the churches in poor countries as important groups whom they can trust and with whom they can work.

Secondly, the church in the Two-Thirds World has many examples of addressing the relationship between human beings, poverty and the environment in a holistic and effective way. My own research studied the work of Bishop Wayan Mastra of the Bali Protestant Church.[3] He built a cathedral in Bali in a garden surrounded by water. There are no walls so that the wind can blow through. It has glass in the roof so that the worshippers can see the fire of the sun. The building integrates worship with creation. The church is placed in a garden because humanity was made in a garden and because Jesus prayed in a garden. He has not made the split which enlightenment Western societies have made between spirit and matter, the individual and society, faith and reason. To people in the Two-Thirds World, the whole of life is religious. Mastra has also begun school assistance programmes, micro-business enterprise schemes among pastors' wives, and work training programmes. He has introduced Balinese music and dress into worship services. He has patronised Balinese Christian artists. Therefore if we say that the problem of the environment is only to do with cutting down the effluents from a factory, we have no room to hear what the Two-Thirds World is telling us about recovering our humanity in relation to creation. They do this by drawing on centuries of spiritual experience in developing that humanity personally and as families. Mastra's practical example shows how Christian faith and practice can affirm and develop the relationship of humanity and the environment in an indigenous culture.

Another striking example is approaches to issues of population. Western techne has made so much of the numbers game that many population control programmes systematically ignore and subvert cultural and religious traditions. Two-Thirds World approaches pay more attention to religion and culture in seeking to change people's practices. Christian faith should assure us that obeying God's will in the present (marital faithfulness) will not undermine his final purposes for creation. Further, it is now recognised that one of the most significant single activities to impact poverty and population is to educate young girls, an area in which Christians have often been pioneers.

Mastra's approach encourages us to develop the religious significance of addressing the gospel to issues of the environment and poverty. We tend to look for solutions from the rich and powerful because they can make things happen. Jesus addressed the poor first. He affirmed that the good news of the liberation he brings is going to be first of all enjoyed and defined by the poor and shared by them with others. Study of Christian ministry among the poor indicates that what is good about the good news to the poor is often first in the area of the self-esteem and worth they are denied in their society. The grace of God in Jesus which enables them to know they are sons and daughters of God in Christ tells those who are counted as nobodies in their societies that they are somebody. They are invited into the covenant community of the church which should communicate to them in practical ways that they are loved, accepted and enabled to be stewards. A particular way of doing this has been through micro-enterprise business development. This approach has grown in partnership with those with access to the world's resources either personally or through trusts and foundations. It is founded in a basic belief that the wealthy and powerful can and should change, and should express that change in a new relationship to the poor.

Christian covenant communities in the West can witness to a different approach to humanity and the environment. The sabbath principle contradicts the notion that we have a duty to maximise our productivity; resources are also given for relaxation, celebration, worship and rest. The tithing, jubilee and gleaning principles similarly contradict the maximisation of efficiency in the use of resources, stipulate that the first tenth and the remainder belong to God and the poor, liberate us from greed for more, and call us to trust in God to provide what we need for life. The loss of God in the consciousness of a society increases the need for intrusiveness into people's affairs so we must also resist the temptation to become advocates for a litigious, audit-based, pharisaic neo-legalism which places impossible burdens on people and removes the area for personal creativity and accountability. We may also reaffirm the Christian doctrine of final judgement at the return of Christ which is preceded by the announcement of judgement with grace in the call for repentance and faith in the face of the secular apocalyptic threats of environmental doom from which there is no salvation save what we might do.

In conclusion, by being fully and joyfully Christian, with the gospel to the poor central to our understanding of the faith, we can bring good news to the environment for which the resurrection of Jesus is the first fruit of the liberation of the whole creation.

Notes

1. World Commission on Environment and Development. *Our Common Future*, Oxford: Oxford University Press, 1987.
2. Professor Lamin Sanneh speaking in a plenary session of Section 2 'Called to Live and Proclaim Good News' of the Lambeth Conference of Anglican Bishops, July 1998, Canterbury, England.
3. Sugden, C. *Seeking the Asian Face of Jesus – The Practice and Theology of Christian Social Witness in Indonesia and India 1974–1996*, Oxford: Regnum, 1997.

Epilogue
John Houghton

> Sir John Houghton FRS is Chairman of The John Ray Initiative[1]
>
> As a result of several questions asked (but not all answered) at the conference, there is an urgent ongoing agenda for Christians – and for The John Ray Initiative in particular – to explore creation care.
>
> **Keywords:** environment, The John Ray Initiative, stewardship, creation

The JRI consultation on 20 February 1999 was a most stimulating day, the discussions being assisted by the wide range of expertise represented amongst those attending. The debate centred on some fundamental themes and concerns that were recognised as suitable topics for further consultation. Towards the end of the afternoon, after the discussions on the individual papers, the authors and the members of the consultation particularly identified some of these main themes and the questions that they raise, namely:

1. Care for the environment is inextricably linked with, and needs to be considered together with, other social and ethical concerns, for instance, poverty, over-use of resources, employment and equity (including international and intergenerational aspects). How, in practical terms, can this integration be brought about and all these concerns be appropriately balanced?

2. What is meant by the 'stewardship' of Creation in a Christian context. Some thought that use of the word 'stewardship' tended to be too anthropocentric and to create a misleading impression regarding our relationship to the environment – although most seemed to agree that it was the best word available. More specific questions relating to stewardship are: what human activity is carried out for the

sake of Creation; what did God intend when he instructed humans to care for Creation; is it not possible to argue that the rest of Creation would be better off without humans? Further, how is the 'image of God' apparent in the relationship of humans to Creation?

3. Can we formulate God's purposes for Creation which are at the basis of our stewardship? These might be, for instance, along the following general lines:

    (a) all parts of Creation should have freedom to act according to their nature or to fulfil their role within Creation;
    (b) the diversity of Creation should be preserved;
    (c) human creativity should be exercised (in what respects is it like God's creativity?) in ways that lead to fulfilment;
    (d) human diversity should be expressed within human communities in loving relationships, again leading to fulfilment;
    (e) human communities should work together towards common goals (which we need to formulate) for the preservation and enhancement of Creation;
    (f) Creation is a training ground for the development of humans including human spirituality.

4. Having formulated such a list of God's purposes in more detail, can we then go on to formulate, for instance, Christian attitudes to work on genetically modified organisms (GMOs) as a worked example?

5. How can we develop meaningful worship of God *for* Creation and more especially *with* Creation?

6. What is the future of Creation – can we develop a meaningful and biblical eschatology of Creation?

7. What relevance have the principles of Christian stewardship to the development of environmentally appropriate

lifestyles and the motivation of environmental action both for Christians and for the secular world?

These and a number of other questions that were raised at the Consultation were not fully answered; for some, answers were not even attempted. They were recognised as important questions which affect both the foundations of our thinking and practical application. It was agreed that the JRI would initiate means, for instance through workshops, to explore them further.

Notes

1. For more details of the activities of The John Ray Initiative, please contact: Dr John Sale, JRI Executive Secretary, Fach Gynan, Moelfre, Oswestry SY10 7QP, United Kingdom. Tel/Fax: +44(01691) 791404. http://www.jri.org.uk. Email: info@jri.org.uk.

TRANSFORMATION

An International Evangelical Dialogue on Mission and Ethics

Editors: Kwame Bediako, Vinay Samuel, Ronald Sider, René Padilla
Associate Editor: Chris Sugden
Assistant Editor: Clare Brignall
Management Consultant: David Stiller
Treasurer: Maranatha Trust (Australia)

Editorial Board:
Tokunboh Adeyemo (General Secretary, Association of Evangelicals of Africa and Madagascar) Kenya/Nigeria; Miriam Adeney (Associate Professor, Seattle Pacific University) USA; Wilson W. Chow (President China Graduate School of Theology) Hong Kong; James M. Dunn (Executive Director, Baptist Joint Committee on Public Affairs) U.S.A.; Samuel Escobar (Professor, Eastern Baptist Theological Seminary) Peru/U.S.A.; Ken Gnanakan (Chairman, Asia Theological Association) India; Kenneth Kantzer (former editor *Christianity Today*) U.S.A.; Peter Kuzmic (President of the Evangelical Theological Faculty, Osijek) Croatia; Lois McKinney (Professor, Trinity, Deerfield) U.S.A.; Emilio Nunez (President, Evangelical Seminary) Guatemala; Clark Pinnock (Professor, McMaster Divinity College) Canada; Bong Rin Ro, Korea; Vinay Samuel (Executive Director, International Fellowship of Evangelical Mission Theologians) India; Ronald Sider (Professor, Eastern Baptist Seminary) U.S.A.; Bong Ho-Son (Professor of Philosophy, Seoul National University) Korea.

Institutional Co-Sponsors:
Associated Mennonite Biblical Seminary; Eastern Baptist Theological Seminary' Eastern College, (Details of institutional co-sponsorship available from the editorial office.)

Editorial Address:
Mss and editorial correspondence should be addressed to Ronald J. Sider at *Transformation*, 6 Lancaster Avenue, Wynnewood, PA 19096, U.S.A. Books for review should be sent to Ronald Sider. Books from Europe may be sent to *Transformation*, P.O. Box 70, Oxford OX2 6HB, Oxford, U.K.

Editorial Policy:
The views expressed in *Transformation* are those of the authors and do not necessarily reflect the viewpoint of the Oxford Centre for Mission Studies.

Subscriptions:
Subscriptions and requests for back numbers should be addressed to the publishers. **All subscriptions from residents in the USA & Canada** should be addressed to Transformation, 6 Lancaster Avenue, Wynnewood, PA 19096, U.S.A. e-mail: esa@esa.mhs.compuserve.com. Elsewhere to: Paternoster Periodicals, P.O. Box 300, Kingstown Broadway, Carlisle, Cumbria CA3 0QS, U.K. Tel: 44-1228-512512; Fax: 44-1228514949

Annual Subscription Rates:
US/Canada: $30.00. U.K.: £16.40. Elsewhere: £17.20. Institutions and residents of the Two-Thirds World, half "Elsewhere" rate. (Long term rates on application to the Publishers).

UK ISSN: 0265-3788

Copyright © Oxford Centre for Mission Studies and the contributors.

Abstracts/Indexing: This journal is abstracted in *Religious and Theological Abstracts*, 121 South College Street (PO Box 215), Myerstown, PA 17067, USA. It is also included in *religion index one: Periodicals (RIO)*. All book reviews are indexed in: *Index to reviews*

in religion (IBBR). Both are available from American Theological Library Association, 820 Church Street, Evanston IL 60201-5613.
E-mail: atla@atla.com.WWW:http:atla.library.vanderbilt.edu/atla/home.html

Microform:
This publication is available on microform from University Microfilms International, 300 N. Zeeb Road, PO Box 1346, Ann Arbor, MI 48106-1346, USA.
Typeset in UK by WestKey, Falmouth, Cornwall. Printed in the UK and published by Paternoster Periodicals, PO Box 300, Carlisle, CA3 0QS, UK (Tel: 44-1228-512512; Fax: 44-1228-514949) on behalf of the Oxford Centre for Mission Studies, P.O. Box 70, Oxford OX2 6HB, UK (Tel: 44-1865-556071; Fax: 44-1865-510823; E-mail: 100270,2155 COMPUSERVE).

Important Note to all Postal Subscribers
When contacting our Subscription Office in Carlisle for any reason
Always quote your Subscriber Reference Number
This appears on the address label used to send your copies to you.

SUBSCRIPTION FORM

Many people read *Transformation* in addition to our subscribers. If you would like to be sure of your copy quarterly, and yourself support this important ministry, do subscribe now.
Details of subscriptions and addresses above.
I enclose payment for TRANSFORMATION
from (dates)..........................
to..............................
Name...
Address...
....
....
Country.............................Postcode........................
Further information from:
Regnum Books International, Oxford Centre for Mission Studies, P.O. Box 70, Oxford OX2 6HB, U.K.

| International telephone: | +44–1865 556071 | UK telephone: | 01865 556071 |
| International fax: | +44–1865 510823 | UK fax: | 01865 510823 |

e-mail: compuserve 100270,2155; Internet:ocms@xc.org

THE·JOHN·RAY·INITIATIVE
connecting environment, science and Christianity

http://www.jri.org.uk   info@jri.org.uk

The *John Ray Initiative* is dedicated to promoting responsible environmental stewardship in accordance with Christian principles and the wise use of science and technology.

Its threefold strategy is to:
- *Refine the message*, developing in cooperation with others a thorough Christian understanding of the environment and how it might be applied and communicated (primarily through consultations and discussion papers)
- *Build a team of JRI Associates* to work with The John Ray Initiative
- *Spread the message*, through courses, workshops, seminars, fact sheets, a website, and speaking at conferences and churches

Contact:
Dr John Sale
JRI Executive Secretary
Fach Gynan
Moelfre
Oswestry SY10 7QP
United Kingdom
Tel/fax: +44(01691)791404
Email: johnsale@aol.com